Empowered Artist

A Call to Action for Musicians, Writers, Visual Artists, and Anyone Who Wants to Make a Difference with Their Creativity

Bob Baker

SORCHA,
YOU ARE SUCH A BRIGHT LIGHT,
KEEP SHINING!

Spotlight Publications
St. Louis, MO

OG
2022

The Empowered Artist

Published by Spotlight Publications and www.Bob-Baker.com
PO Box 28441, St. Louis, MO 63146 USA
(314) 329-1395 • bob@bob-baker.com

ISBN-13: 978-1514215111
ISBN-10: 151421511X

Disclaimer

This book is designed to provide information and inspiration for musicians, writers, artists, and other creative people. It is sold with the understanding that the publisher and author are not engaged in rendering legal, accounting, or other professional services. If legal or other expert assistance is required, the services of a competent professional should be sought.

It is not the purpose of this book to cover the full range of information that is otherwise available on this topic, but instead to complement, amplify, and supplement other texts. You are urged to read all available material and tailor the information to your individual needs.

Every effort has been made to make this book as accurate as possible. However, there may be mistakes, and some details may be inaccurate by the time you read this. Therefore, this text should be used only as a general guide and not as the ultimate source of information on the topic.

The author and publisher shall have neither liability nor responsibility to any person or entity with respect to any loss or damage caused, or alleged to have been caused, directly or indirectly, by the information contained in this book.

Free Gifts for You!

As a special thank you for purchasing this book, I want to give you FREE access to my $99.00 course, "**30 Ways to Become an Empowered Artist**."

You'll get more than three hours of online video training, worksheets, and more.

I'll also send you a FREE sample of my book, ***The DIY Career Manifesto****: The Unconventional Guide to Turning Your Talents and Know-How Into a Profitable Business*.

Go here to claim these free gifts now:

www.DIYcareerManifesto.com

What About Bob?

Bob Baker is on a mission to help musicians, authors and creative entrepreneurs of all kinds use their talents and know-how to make a living and make a difference in the world.

He is the author of the highly acclaimed *Guerrilla Music Marketing Handbook* and several other books, including *The DIY Career Manifesto*, *55 Ways to Promote & Sell Your Book on the Internet*, *Unleash the Artist Within*, and *Branding Yourself Online*. He also developed the "Music Marketing 101" course at Berkleemusic, the online continuing education division of Berklee College of Music.

Bob is an active musician, workshop leader, visual artist, actor, and former music magazine editor who teaches creative people how to get exposure, connect with fans, and increase their incomes through their artistic passions.

Since 1995 Bob has published "The Buzz Factor" ezine, one of the first music tips email newsletters in existence. He was one of the early proponents of musicians, writers, and other creative people taking their careers into their own hands and not relying on industry gatekeepers to save them.

Visit **www.TheBuzzFactor.com, www.FullTimeAuthor.com, www.DIYcareerManifesto.com** and **www.Bob-Baker.com** for more details.

Contents

Cover photo credits: The guitar player image on the left, compliments of www.SplitShire.com. The photographer image in the middle is by Wil Stewart via www.Stocksnap.io. The photo of painter Flora Bowley on the right is by Zipporah Lomax, www.ZipporahLomax.com.

Thanks to Phia Lynne for the sharp editing eye.

To Pooki, for empowering me with
your unconditional love!

Foreword

During the long years when I had the nagging suspicion that I was not anywhere close to living the life of my dreams, I had no clue that I already possessed something that would make such a thing possible. Inevitable, in fact. This powerful force was my own entrepreneurial spirit which, happily, had survived years of neglect until I was ready to recognize it and put it to work.

Like others who had made the same discovery, I came to realize that this is the sleeping giant that resides within all of us. Whether or not we awaken it is completely up to us.

So what is entrepreneurial spirit anyway? I think it's more than just the catalyst for working on your own. It's an approach to life. It's living every day with the attitude of an explorer. It's being enthusiastic about problem-solving. It's being alert to opportunity. It's an active and wildly creative way of making your own unique contribution to the world.

And then you get paid on top of that!

We see entrepreneurial spirit in immigrant business owners and teenagers who start a rock band. We see it in mothers who invent a better baby carrier and in young adults finding new ways to use the Internet. We see it when Heifer International gives a flock of animals to a family in a Third World country. In fact, millions of people throughout the world are claiming their own entrepreneurial spirit and putting it to work every day.

Nevertheless, it remains an endangered species in many of us. Several years ago, my younger sister left a corporate job she had held for 25 years to start her own business. For the first year, every time I saw her she'd ask, "Is it really okay to get paid to have so much fun?"

Of course, I assured her it was perfectly acceptable. At the same time, I realized that she and I were not the only ones who had gotten a strong message growing up that we shouldn't expect work and fun to coexist.

That's where the message of *The Empowered Artist* can be so valuable in helping you get past old, tired beliefs and attitudes you may not even know you possess. Bob Baker is the perfect teacher on this journey, since he's been creatively self-employed for years. Best of all, he's been paying attention to his own journey and shares his discoveries with anyone smart enough to listen.

After all, every entrepreneur soon discovers that success is truly a collection of lots of little steps and tiny bits of personal growth that conspire together to make up the foundation of a life worth living. Therefore, take your time as you explore the principles in this book.

 "Good for the body is the work of the body, and good for the soul is the work of the soul, and good for either is the work of the other," said Henry David Thoreau. No wonder those folks who lived through the Italian Renaissance accomplished so much. I always think that their unspoken motto was something like, "Make love. Make art. Make music. Make business. Make a difference." There's much to learn from that example here in the 21st century.

Quite simply, there is no shortage of opportunity for innovative thinking backed up by creative activity. *The Empowered*

Artist will stimulate both. It's a road map that can take you in directions you haven't yet imagined.

It also comes with bonuses you might not have considered possible. As your own entrepreneurial spirit burns brighter, you'll be inspiring and awakening other sleeping giants around you.

Create. Love. Serve. The assignments don't get any better than that.

-**Barbara J. Winter**, author of *Making a Living Without a Job* and publisher of the *Winning Ways* newsletter

Welcome to the Empowered Artist Movement

You hold in your hands a book that may very well shake up your perspective on the role that artists play in society. If you are a musician, writer, visual artist, designer, performer, or any other type of creative person ... that means YOU!

My goal is to awaken the boundless creative potential that resides within you, and to remind you of the incredible value you bring to the world through your artistic skills.

In case you think my ambitions are a bit over the top, allow me to test your knowledge of history for a moment.

Does the name Piero Soderini sound familiar? How about Georges-Eugene Haussmann?

If those names do ring a bell, that means you must be a student of European history. Congratulations. If you don't recognize them, don't feel bad. Most people have no clue.

What if I were to ask you the same question about the names Da Vinci, Michelangelo, Monet, Renoir, or Van Gogh?

Most likely, you know them all, even though these historic figures have not been alive for 100 to 500 years. They are names recognized by millions of people around the world, and I didn't even use their full names.

Let's get back to the two people I started this history lesson with ...

Piero Soderini was elected in 1502 to a government position known as the gonfaloniere of the Republic of Florence. He was a prominent statesman in what is now known as Italy.

Two years into Soderini's term, 28-year-old Michelangelo completed a massive statue called David, one of the art world's most acclaimed sculptures. Around the same time a multitalented fellow named Leonardo Da Vinci began working on a painting that would be known the world over as the Mona Lisa.

Fast forward to the mid 1800s, when Georges-Eugene Haussmann became the prefect of the Seine in France. He was selected by Napoleon III to oversee a massive expansion of Paris. Haussmann's influence on the city is still being felt. Yet, not many people are really aware of him today.

Around that same time in Paris, a rogue group of visual artists were exploring new approaches to painting. Some of them included Claude Monet, Pierre-Auguste Renoir, and Vincent Van Gogh.

Will the real influencers please stand up!

Why is it that all these centuries later, Soderini and Haussmann are a fading memory of history, while the impact and popularity of the aforementioned artists remains high?

You know the answer.

Because throughout history it is artists that have had the greatest impact on society. Seriously, what comes to mind when you think of the great civilizations of the past? Is it the politicians and military leaders who were well-known (and often feared) in their day? Well, in some instances, yes.

But I think you'll agree that it is the architecture, art, music, poetry, fashion, and literary works of each era and location that are remembered and admired in far greater numbers.

The examples to support this are seemingly endless: Shakespeare, Dickens, Hemingway, Mozart, Cassatt, O'Keefe, Warhol, Sinatra, Presley, Angelou, Plath, Rowling, Lloyd Wright, da le Renta, Chanel, Lennon and McCartney. (Again, I'm using only the last name of each person, but I bet you know immediately who most of them are.)

Make no mistake. Creative people have a long history of making a difference in the world. Most innovation and human progress over the centuries has come from human beings who think like artists.

But for some reason, the role of the artist has become diluted, and even frowned upon, in many cultures. This has lead to the stigma of the "starving artist" and the phrase "don't quit your day job."

I'm on a mission to eradicate these misguided notions and restore musicians, writers, and artists to their proper status – as a thriving community of people who wield great cultural, political and economic power.

This isn't just wishful thinking on my part. There's even a book called *The Cultural Creatives: How 50 Million People Are Changing the World* that chronicles this monumental shift in modern society.

One way I'm addressing this widespread artist identity crisis is through this *Empowered Artist* book. In the pages that follow you'll find short, kick-in-the-pants principles designed to inspire you to wake up and realize your potential and true value as a creative person.

How do you define "Empowered Artist"?

Of course, I will shed light on the many layers of this "empowered" concept throughout the book, but let me offer a taste of how I define it here.

Being an Empowered Artist (a term I will always capitalize throughout this book for emphasis) means you approach your art with a sense of confidence and pride. It means you don't apologize or feel unworthy because you feel called to pursue a creative endeavor or livelihood.

It means you don't write yourself off as having a frivolous notion of doing something significant with your gifts. Being an Empowered Artist means you don't water down your ambitions or let your sensitivity work against you.

That doesn't mean you will never feel doubt, uncertainty or fear. Anyone who pursues any vocation feels those negative emotions, no matter how traditional a career path they choose. But artists seem burdened more than they should with these self-imposed hurdles. When you adopt the Empowered Artist mindset, you keep them in their proper place and life gets easier.

When you become empowered you can choose how creativity fits into your life. You can make solid decisions on whether to pursue your craft as a hobby, part-time or full-time activity. It allows you to come to these decisions based on rational thought, instead of being influenced by insecurity or what society insists you ought to do.

Believe me, being an Empowered Artist is a much better place to be.

To clarify, my motivation in writing this book isn't just to make a few musicians, writers, and painters feel good about themselves. That's thinking too small. *My vision is to change the world!*

Are you with me?

The Truth About Living a Rich, Creative Life

I've been blessed to have made a living most of my life from my creative endeavors. If you don't mind, I'd like to use this section to let you know who I am and why I'm so dedicated to the Empowered Artist cause.

I can trace my interests in music and writing back to grade school. By my teenage years I was playing in rock bands and writing an occasional short story in my spare time.

In my early twenties I supported myself as a full-time musician for a few years. In my late twenties I started publishing a magazine that covered the local music scene in my hometown of St. Louis, Missouri. That was the first time I combined my twin interests in music and the written word.

I published the magazine for ten years, learned a lot about being a member of the media, honed my chops at writing and editing, had a great time, and eked out a living doing it.

During this phase of my life I also immersed myself in a wide array of creative activities. I acted in plays, directed plays, did standup comedy, formed improv comedy troupes, wrote and performed sketch comedy, dabbled in acrylic painting, and continued to write, record and perform original music.

I admit, I was a little nuts when it came to all the stuff I was interested in. If something seemed like it would be fun to do, I found a way to experience it – sooner rather than later. And I usually found a way to make at least a little money from most of the creative things I did.

Don't think for a moment that I accomplished all of this because I have a highly driven, Type-A personality. Hardly. I'm pretty laid back. When I was younger I was even quite shy in social situations and lacked confidence. (Sound familiar?) But I found a way to pursue my interests despite these shortcomings.

A turning point

In my early thirties my first book was published. It was a guide on how to make money in the music business. That was a turning point for me, as I made a decision to focus my efforts on being an author, teacher and speaker.

Based on the feedback I got from the readers of my book and music magazine, I knew I had a gift for imparting information in a conversational, easy-to-digest manner. I saw this as the best way I could contribute to society and make a living at the same time.

I got on the Internet in 1995 and over the ensuing years used this wonderful digital gateway to the world to spread my message, promote my books, and build my reputation as an author. I was one of the first people to self-publish books and resources on music marketing for independent artists.

As a result of being online early and consistently publishing articles, blog posts, podcasts, and videos clips for years on end ... I've earned a reputation as a pioneer of sorts on the topics of music marketing and digital information publishing.

Yes, I have worked part-time and full-time jobs here and there throughout my life. The last time I worked for someone else was 2004. I quit that job with the goal of remaining self-employed for the rest of my life.

Since I've had a bit of success as an author, I also created a secondary niche for writers and independent book publishers. More recently I've expanded my audience to also include what I call "creative entrepreneurs" of all kinds. Each niche has a line of books, audio programs, workshops, and online courses. It makes sense for me to address these various audiences, since I continue to be involved in so many different creative endeavors.

My activities as an author, speaker and teacher pay the bills. I also supplement my income by playing music, selling my original paintings, teaching and performing improv comedy, and more.

The bottom line is, I know first-hand what it's like to live a rich, creative life. I also know there are countless others around the world who would like to do the same thing, but they convince themselves that it is not possible.

Getting inspired

Over the years I've also had the good fortune to interview hundreds of successful musicians, authors, artists, and more. While sharing these interviews with my audience, I was also inspired by them. I took the best practices that my guests revealed and applied them to my own career. I noticed some consistent habits and traits that these successful creative people had. This also made me realize the missing ingredients that plague the majority of artists.

For reasons I may never quite understand, since a young age I felt compelled to express and share my creativity. I didn't really have role models or mentors who encouraged me. It was just something I've always felt the need to do.

I'm not suggesting it was easy. I faced the same pressures as you do from people who carry the misguided "starving artist" and "struggling artist" banner. I had to stubbornly pursue my creative path, experiment, fail, and try again – over and over – to find ways to make it work.

And I did indeed find a way – as have thousands of other creative types, despite what you hear to the contrary.

However, most people don't live their lives this way. They ignore their soul's calling. They muffle their innate urge to be creative. They deny themselves – and the world – the benefit of their gifts.

And I am on a mission to right this wrong!

That's who I am. That's why I wrote this book. And that's why you should read it and embody the principles contained in these pages.

Before You Dive In ...

Now you know why this book exists and who created it, here are a few more details before we jump into the meat of the material.

Not everyone is at the same stage of their creative journey. It's not always easy to categorize, but I bet you fit into one of these four basic levels:

- You have an interest in the arts and are considering getting more involved. You're not sure where it fits into your life yet, but you're eager to explore the possibilities.
- You are already somewhat involved in music, writing, visual art or some other form of creative expression. You feel a strong calling to pursue it and are wondering if you should step up your efforts and immerse yourself more fully.
- You are actively engaged in your craft and maybe even earning a part-time income from it. You love the idea of growing your sideline art activities into a full-time career, and you're looking for indications that this is a smart path to take.
- You are already making a living in the arts. People admire you and your work and you generate a decent income from it. Now you're ready to get inspired and take things to the next level.

No matter where you are in your evolution as an artist, writer or performer, you could probably use a little more fuel to power your efforts. Therefore, if you can relate to any of the categories above, you will find a wealth of useful wisdom in the pages that follow.

What this book is and isn't

The Empowered Artist is designed to be a kick in the pants, a call to action, and a rallying cry for you to step into your greatness. While we will cover a lot of specific action steps you should take, this is NOT a comprehensive book about how to build a business. I have published many resources over the years on marketing, and this book touches on that topic, but that's not the main content you will find here.

This book also doesn't delve deeply into any one particular creative discipline. It's not solely geared toward musicians or writers or visual artists, etc. This is a shared journey that all creative people, no matter what specialty they are drawn to, can benefit from.

Therefore, throughout the book I'll make references to music, art, writing, dance, poetry, design, fashion, filmmaking and more. However, in an effort to be more concise, many times I'll simply refer to your "art." Just know that, in this context, the word *art* refers to anything you produce in the creative realm. Got it?

What we will do in this book is immerse ourselves in a big dose of reality checks, empowering attitudes, shifting perspectives, powerful mindsets, and nitty-gritty details on the real work you need to do to make a difference (and make a living) with your talents and know-how.

The reason so many struggle with creative ambitions is because they lack these rock-bottom principles. To truly thrive in the arts you must instill these big picture ideals into your creative DNA.

That's what this book is: *a transfusion of success principles for modern day artists.*

Also, every section ends with a Call to Action – an affirmative step you can take to tell yourself (and the world) that you mean business, that you are here to make your creative mark.

The world needs you and the gifts that only you are uniquely qualified to deliver. We need you to live up to your potential, to shine your light, to step into your greatness.

I hope you're ready. Let's begin.

The Foundation: Ten Guiding Principles You Should Internalize to Become an Empowered Artist

1) Approve yourself

One of the main reasons creative people are not more empowered is because they often cultivate a general sense of unworthiness. As a result, the doubts and questions flow:

- What will people think?
- Why am I pursuing this risky, crazy pipe dream to begin with?
- Who am I to follow in the footsteps of the truly great artists who have come before me?
- Won't I starve to death or end up begging for money on street corners?

Stop it already. Please! You sound pathetic when you say these things (even when the voice is only in your head).

Just think if you thought that way every time you brushed your teeth or tied your shoes:

- What if I accidentally choke on the toothbrush?
- What if the toothpaste has been poisoned?
- What if I inadvertently kick myself while putting on my shoes?
- What if I break my finger (or worse, my neck) in a horrific lacing accident?

Doesn't this sound ridiculous? Of course, it does.

One way artists try to subdue these negative feelings is to gain credibility. They often seek out some form of officially sanctioned approval. Doing so, they think, will appease their family and friends, the nasty voices in their heads, and even the Gods.

So they take classes, pursue degrees, get certified, study with established mentors, or jump through countless academic hoops in order to earn a couple of letters to follow their names.

There's nothing inherently wrong with these things – as long as they're done with an intention to hone your skills. But when the underlying motivation is to prop up your self-worth as an artist, the results fall short.

Here's the bottom line: You don't need anyone's approval to be fully worthy of pursuing your creative desires (on whatever level you choose). The fact that you feel a calling to do it is all the reason you need.

That doesn't mean you're guaranteed fame or fortune simply because you have an interest in something (more on this later), but you most definitely are as worthy as anyone to give it a shot.

If you are drawn to a creative endeavor, if have any inkling to pursue something artistic ... respect and nurture that impulse. You owe it to yourself to act on it.

Don't wait for approval. Don't wait to be accepted. Don't wait to be chosen or picked.

Give yourself permission. It's the only green light you need to get started on your path to being an Empowered Artist.

Call to Action

Write down this affirmation and read it out loud:

"I give myself permission to pursue my creative callings. I am worthy to follow these artistic urges as much as I am worthy to breathe the air around me. This is who I am and what I am being called to do. And I owe it to myself and the world to fully explore it."

Really read this and do your best to internalize the message, even if it feels awkward at first. Especially if it feels awkward. You may be trying on a new attitude that you've never worn before. But keep trying it on. Over time you will relax into it and feel right at home.

2) Bask in amazement

I remember many years ago when it struck me. I'm not even sure what sparked the idea. But it was profound.

The thing that astounded me was the realization that everything I created (whether it was a song, a short story, a comedy sketch, or a painting) started as an idea in my mind. It began as an intangible spark of inspiration.

Then, through physical action in the 3D world, that idea became a real thing – a painting someone could hang on a wall, a story someone could read, a song someone could hear, a theatrical performance someone could watch and enjoy.

I was blown away by that expanded awareness of the power of imagination. And I still am. Are you?

Of course, I didn't have exclusive rights to this process. Every manmade item was created in exactly this way. Chairs, tables, cars, light bulbs, mobile phones, hair dryers, toilet paper, and soap. Everything started as an idea in someone's mind.

Equally eye opening was the realization that none of these ideas would have become tangible things if someone had not taken additional steps. For any object to come into existence, the original inspiration must be acted upon.

The person who conceived the idea must either write it down, create a sketch or blueprint, record it, perform it, build it, or at least communicate it to another human being who can take action on it.

Ideas alone die on the vine. But ideas coupled with action produce tangible results. It's a simple concept to grasp, but that doesn't make it any less amazing.

Therefore, if your goal is to be an Empowered Artist, you will help your cause by maintaining a sense of awe about the artistic process you engage in. It isn't a frivolous game. It's a miraculous act of creation. And you are fortunate enough to be an active participant.

Call to Action

Spend five minutes thinking about something that either you or an artist you admire has created. Consider the steps that had to be taken for the final product to come into existence. From the initial idea to the many actions that were taken along the way to the eventual manifestation of the song, book, painting, or whatever it is.

Cultivate a sense of amazement over this process. Feel deeply grateful for being able to take part in this divine dance of imagination, action, skill and determination.

3) Prioritize your art

Think about the things you actually got done today or yesterday or over the past week. While I'm sure your list includes some spontaneous activities, I'm guessing most of the things you accomplished were planned.

If you had a doctor's appointment, got the oil changed in your car, met a friend for coffee, or picked up the kids from school … most likely you knew about it ahead of time and planned your schedule around these events. And that's as it should be.

Sadly, most people who claim they want to do more with their creativity take a very different approach. Painting, writing, rehearsing, and designing are relegated to a fantasyland category referred to as "when I have time to get around to it."

Sorry, but that's not going to earn you Empowered Artist status.

Your art is important, isn't it? Then why not give it the prominence it deserves?

If you're a parent, imagine your nine-year-old daughter saying, "Can you give me a ride home after soccer practice tonight?" Would your reply be, "Well, I'll try to bring you home tonight if I can get around to it"?

Or how would you respond to a friend you haven't seen in years who is asking to meet for lunch on Thursday? Would you say, "Well, let's see how things go that day. If I feel inspired to do it, I'll show up"?

Of course, you wouldn't do that. Your child's needs and safety are too precious. Your relationship with your friend is too important to treat so frivolously. You honor those commitments with the respect they deserve.

So why not treat your creative activities with the same level of significance?

The main reason your art doesn't get enough attention is because it is usually worked in around other things. You get to it only after the "important" tasks are completed, and only if you have the energy and inspiration left to devote to it. Cultivating your gifts are given second- or third-class status on your to-do list.

Empowered Artists give creative time the same priority as car maintenance, doctor visits, home repairs, and obligations to friends and family members. You know how important your art is. Give it the red carpet, first-class treatment it deserves!

Call to Action

The best way to make sure your creative time gets attention is to put it on the calendar. If you don't have specific times etched out during your week to devote to your craft, it will rarely happen on its own.

So look at the calendar and think about your average week. When could you carve out some time for your creativity? Could you get up a little earlier on certain mornings? Could you squeeze in time on certain afternoons or evenings? What about Saturday morning or Sunday night?

Determine the best times to work on your art. Put those blocks of time – no matter how short or long they are – on your weekly calendar. And don't just pencil them in. Write them in indelible ink!

Then treat them with the same respect and commitment you give to all of your other obligations. Because developing your talent is damn important!

4) Put fear and uncertainty in their place

Do you know where the richest place on earth is? It's not Wall Street or Silicon Valley or Beverly Hills.

It's the graveyard.

Why? Because, as Les Brown explains, "that's where you'll find all the hopes and dreams that were never fulfilled, the books that were never written, the songs that were never sung, the inventions that were never shared, and the cures that were never discovered."

What a sobering thought. And sadly, it's true.

The reason so many people fall short of their potential is because of that nasty F-word, "Fear," as well as its corruptive cousin, "Uncertainly."

These twin culprits have stopped more great ideas, works of art, literary classics, and timeless songs than any repressive regime ever has. And they have no doubt stopped you in your creative tracks too. These clever, conniving rascals come in all shapes and sizes: fear of failure, fear of success, fear of ridicule, and fear of poverty, to name but a few.

From the "uncertainty" side of the tracks we get such inner dialogue classics as:

- But I don't know how to pull that off
- What will really happen if I pursue this?
- How will I make enough money doing this?
- What if I'm just not that good at it?

It can be frightening and overwhelming. And this leads a lot of potential artists to draw this conclusion: People who "make it" in the arts must have learned to banish fear and slay the uncertainty monster. The "chosen few" have a special gift that shelters them from these two evil thought demons.

Which leads to the disempowering idea: "I am obviously missing the fearless gene, so I'm not cut out for this path."

Please allow me to set the record straight:

That is absolute hogwash! (I'm not even sure what hogwash is, but it seems like the appropriate word to throw in here.) Stop deluding yourself with this Super Artist Fear and Uncertainty Deflector Shield notion.

The truth is, every artist – no, let's make that every person who is alive and conscious – has regular, reoccurring feelings of fear and uncertainty. It goes with the territory of being human, although creative people do seem to be affected by it more than most.

So, those talented artists you look up to have not learned to banish fear and uncertainty. They have not silenced them. Instead, they have learned to carry on in spite of them. They manage to put them in their place and lower the volume knob of resistance they create.

If you are serious about being an Empowered Artist, you will learn to do the same.

Call to Action

The best way to reduce the power that fear and uncertainty have over you is to diminish their standing. What stops you is treating them like royalty. What holds you back is believing that they are the unquestionable authority on your life.

To put fear and uncertainty in their place, you must disrespect them – not treat them like parents who you can never disobey. So tell them to pipe down or, God forbid, to "shut the hell up!"

Would you like a fun and creative way to deal with them? Give them a silly name. Would you really take advice from an entity named Jethro or Trixie? Give them a ridiculous cartoon voice, so you can't possibly take their nonsensical ramblings seriously. Imagine that their voices are coming from a giant stuffed animal or a circus clown (the funny ones, not the scary clowns).

When all else fails, get all Harry Potter on their asses and call out the secret spell, lift the magic sword, and slay those dragons into smithereens.

That's how you put fear and uncertainty in their place!

5) Wonder why

Throughout this book you will notice some reoccurring themes. We will address some topics many times from different angles, and that's by design. Here's why: As a creative person, you face a myriad of obstacles, most of which are self-imposed. These hurdles were created by repeatedly buying into certain ideas and beliefs that simply don't serve you well in your pursuit of Empowered Artist status.

You won't overcome a lifetime of these cognitive barriers by reading a myth-busting concept once. Some of these mental obstacles are so deeply ingrained, it will take repeated exposures to new ways of thinking to dislodge them.

So let's address another defeating mindset related to your worth and confidence as an artist. The good news is, the cure is as simple as adding an extra word to a common phrase.

Whether you use this exact term or not, and whether you say it aloud or quietly to yourself, you often ask this simple question:

Why me?

It seems so harmless, but the underlining belief is, once again, based on fear and doubt and wondering if you are worthy. It stems from you questioning your ability to step into the role of writer, painter, musician, actor, or whatever your calling is.

As I emphasized in the previous section, your goal is not to eliminate fear-based thoughts. Don't beat yourself up because you momentarily feel off kilter or confused. That goes with the territory.

To become an Empowered Artist you must upset the pattern, break the code, tip over the unworthiness apple cart. You must slowly replace the "why me?" notions with more positive alternatives.

It's not always easy. It takes time to fully ingrain. But it is well worth the effort to upgrade your mental operating system.

Call to Action

This one is simple. The next time you find yourself muttering "Why me?" – translation: "Who am I to think I am an artist?" – do this: Add the word "not."

Yes, "not" is a negative word when used by itself. But when added to the middle of the phrase, it transforms it into a powerful question.

Here's your new mantra: "Why not me?"

And why not indeed? Do you think that every successful artist started out at the top of the heap? Do you think everyone you look up to came out of the womb with a stellar reputation?

Nope. They all had to earn it. They all had to start from the bottom. They all had to figure it out for themselves. They all had to work their way out of obscurity and into greater prominence.

So ask yourself, "Why not me?" Even though you're not entitled to automatic success, you have as much potential to thrive with your art as anyone. See that as your destiny. Own that outcome. Move toward that vision for your life.

Every month there is a new crop of writers, musicians and artists that makes waves, gets exposure, and hits the bestseller lists. That's a fact. In the months and years ahead, someone is going to break through and make an impact in your area of creativity.

Which begs the question ...

Why not YOU?

6) Strike a balance

We've spent a lot of time in these early sections addressing self-worth and self-confidence. This is vitally important work that every artist must address to truly step into their power.

This is also a great time to point out the danger of going to extremes with this new attitude adjustment. When I stress the importance of giving yourself permission to succeed and putting fear and uncertainly in their place, I am not suggesting that you be overly boastful or cocky or full of yourself. That's a sure way to turn people off and stunt your career in the arts, not expand it.

Clarification: This is a subject I will explore delicately, because what I'm saying can be taken the wrong way, depending on where you rank on the self-confidence scale.

There are people in the world who think highly of themselves to the point of making everyone around them nauseous. They think the world owes them something simply because they exist, and they are shocked that every door they knock on doesn't automatically open with great fanfare.

If you fall into this category (and if you do, you probably don't even realize it), then you are more prone to take my empowerment advice and abuse it. You will absorb this worthiness topic and give yourself permission to think you're better than everyone else. You'll wonder why there are so many clueless people who fail to see your genius.

The key point: You don't want to be a pompous artist. The real goal is to transform yourself into an Empowered Artist, and that's a far different thing.

While there are many people who lean toward this ego-driven temperament (and we have all experienced them), I contend that the vast majority of potential artists gravitate toward the "lacking in confidence" side of the scale. They sell themselves short and downplay the impact that their art can have on others.

And it's this "I'm not worthy" demographic that the majority of this book is written for. So, if you fall into the "why me?" category, please don't read this section and overcompensate. Don't think I'm saying you had better tone down your ambitions, that you should dim the light that is aching to shine from you.

The main message here is to embody your newfound confidence with humility and with a sense of vulnerability. You can feel worthy and still not come off as overly boastful. Or, as the subtitle of Peggy Klaus' book *Brag!* states, you should "toot your own horn without blowing it."

Call to Action

Read the following paragraphs, then take a few minutes to visualize how living in this balanced manner would empower you as an artist:

Think of your confidence and sense of artistic self-worth as an internal quality. It's something that resides within you as a foundational part of your being. You feel in your core that you have a right to pursue your passions and you know that, once honed and let loose on the planet, your gifts have the potential to change lives and benefit a lot of people.

Meanwhile, on your exterior you carry a quiet confidence in who you are and what you are meant to do. You don't come off as apologetic or uncertain. You don't downplay the creative skill you are engaged in. At the same time, you don't come off as being abrasive, boastful or overbearing.

People are attracted to your enthusiasm for your craft. You aren't shy about promoting and selling your work, but you also let the quality of your work do much of the talking. On a daily basis, you practice the delicate balance of being confident and humble at the same time.

Wouldn't that be a great way to live and move in the world?

7) Know your mode

There's a fun exercise called "The eagle and the jackhammer" that I do at some of my live workshops. I get eight to ten people up and split them into two groups. With one group I take a minute or two and have them close their eyes and imagine that they are eagles, soaring majestically through the sky. Then I ask them to physically move in tandem with the feeling of flying like an eagle.

Then I move to the other group and ask them to visualize that they are jackhammers, powerfully breaking through concrete and pummeling their way into the ground. I also ask them to get physical and move their bodies like jackhammers.

Next, I switch gears. I ask the first group to continue to imagine that they are eagles but to move their bodies like jackhammers. With the second group (you guessed it) I instruct them to visualize being a jackhammer in their minds while moving like a soaring eagle.

The resulting visual is a hoot for the rest of the workshop attendees who watch from the comfort of their seats. Bodies spasm, faces contort, and equilibriums are frantically off balance.

Besides pushing the volunteers out of their comfort zones, there's a bigger point to this exercise. When you think and visualize one thing, while simultaneously acting out something entirely different, you get off kilter. You feel disoriented. You lose control.

It's a great analogy for the way many creative people pursue their art. In their minds they may think that they are headed toward professional status with their craft; but their day-to-day actions are more aligned with a part-time hobby mode. They may think that they want to make a full-time income from their talents; but their habits are more consistent with having fun or making a difference than with making a living.

I believe that's where a lot of the "struggling and starving artist" rap comes from. It's the ill-fated result of operating from conflicting modes. Just like the jackhammers that can't reconcile being eagles at the same time, artists go through life off balance and unstable.

So, where do you stand? What mode are you operating from, both mentally and physically?

The purpose of this book isn't just to make you a full-time, professional artist. The real mission is to make you an Empowered Artist, no matter what mode you choose to pursue. But whatever that mode is, it's crucial that you be honest with yourself and make a decision on where art fits into your life at this time. And then make certain that your thoughts and deeds support that decision.

You can be either an eagle or a jackhammer. But life gets a lot more challenging when you attempt to be both at the same time.

Call to Action

Get out a notebook or journal. Write down some honest notes to yourself about the role that your creative gift (music, art, literature, dance, design, etc.) plays in your life.

How much of your time would you ideally like to devote to your craft? A few hours a month? Fifteen hours a week? Six hours a day, five days a week?

Also, what are your income goals? Is making money not a factor at all? Is simply sharing your art most important? Or would you prefer to make some supplemental, sideline income? Or is your ultimate goal to make a substantial full-time income from your craft?

Why this exercise is so important: The way you spend your days will be much different if full-time, professional status is your goal, compared to your actions in part-time hobby mode – and vice versa. You have to be in alignment with yourself to be a truly Empowered Artist.

There's no right or wrong answer here. The most important thing is to know your mode at this time in your life, and then to think and act accordingly. You can always change your mind and evolve later. But knowing where you stand now will make your life a lot easier.

8) Close the gap

No matter what mode you choose, no matter what role you decide art plays in your life, I bet the ideal vision you hold for your creative life is different from your current reality. It might be just a tad different or it could seem like an ocean separates where you are from where you want to be.

And that's a fantastic realization to have. It means you have vision and ambition. It means you are growth-oriented. It means you are willing to look ahead and imagine a brighter future. However, the real question is: How will you respond to the gap?

If you ask *dis*empowered artists what their plans are, they'll tell you all about their current struggles and lackluster results. They'll tell you what's wrong and how it's always been that way. They won't speak of growth or evolution or what they are working toward.

They are stuck in the muck of what is.

On the other end of the spectrum are the dreamers who imagine possibilities. They visualize and affirm their success. They mentally and spiritually prop themselves up. That all sounds good until you discover that their actions and behavior do not support the vision. It's another case of mixed career modes – thinking one thing and doing (or not doing) another.

These good people have their heads in the clouds and have lost their footing on the ground.

One thing I credit for my own success in the arts is being able to recognize and acknowledge both ends of the spectrum. I have ambitions and visualize the success I desire. Yet, I am also keenly aware of the reality of my current situation. I clearly see the disparity between the two points – where I am vs. where I want to be.

For many artists, being aware of this gap (which is often a seemingly monumental one) creates frustration. It leads to feelings of helplessness and weakness. It causes some otherwise talented people to throw up their hands and give up.

At times the disparity has had the same negative impact on me. It can be depressing to realize how far short of the goal line you are. But I've found ways to minimize the impact and actually use the gap to inspire me.

I'll cover one helpful strategy in the Call to Action. For now, allow me to give you another perspective on the tension that can creep up when you are keenly aware of the gap. It all comes down to how you respond to the disparity. As I said before, many artists give up and feel it's too much of a struggle. That is one way you can choose to deal with it.

What works best for me is using the tension created by the gap as fuel to shorten the distance. It helps if you have a stubborn side of you that rears its determined head at times like these. I get to a point where I just won't settle for my current status as my eternal state any longer. Nothing is fixed in time. Things change constantly. Why couldn't they change in a manner that supports you?

So, for me, the key to releasing the tension of the gap is to take action and move. To figure out what I can do on a daily basis, little by little, to close the gap. Might this same strategy work for you?

Call to Action

There's one proven method to closing the gap that successful people throughout history have cited as the reason they get things done. I'm sure you've heard it before. If you have, here it is again.

One of the best ways to close the gap between where you are and where you desire to be is to break down the process into baby steps. The gap creates so much frustration because of the seeming immensity of it. How will you ever cross that chasm? It seems so daunting.

The solution: Stop looking at the entire distance and focus only on the next small step! Don't overwhelm yourself. What's the next tiny action you can take today? What's the next little milestone? That's all you need to concern yourself with for now.

Let's say you want to drive from Pittsburgh, Pennsylvania, to Chicago, Illinois. You don't have to think about Cleveland, Toledo, South Bend, Chicago and every point in between all at the same time. Just put your energy into getting to Cleveland first. Then you can worry about the next leg of the trip.

To close the gap, be stubborn and determined about where you are going, and put most of your attention on the next little step you will take to get there.

9) Ask better questions

Whether you are aware of it or not, you are always asking yourself questions. Your mind is a veritable question-producing machine.

- What should I have for breakfast?
- Where should I take my new client to lunch tomorrow?
- How should I drive to the gig to avoid the highway construction traffic?
- What is causing that funny smell?
- Why does my hair look so damn good today?

Luckily, your brain is also an answer-producing machine. It operates much like a computer processor. Every time you submit a question for consideration, your brain assumes it is a valid data input, and it goes to work in search of a valid answer.

This is a wonderful human ability. And amazingly, your brain starts feeding back answers within seconds of your mind posing a new question.

But here's the thing: You can allow this miraculous process to take place on autopilot, as most people do. Or, you can be more conscious and purposeful with the way you use it. Thankfully, I learned long ago that there are empowering and disempowering ways to use the questions and answers that our minds generate.

Here are examples of weak questions that artists often ask themselves:

- Why can't I get a break?
- Why doesn't anyone care about my art?
- Why is this local arts scene so lame?
- Why can't I sell any of my paintings (or books or music, etc.)?

When presented with such questions, your brain (being the computer-like organ that it is) goes to work searching for specific answers to your specific questions. The information that comes racing back at you probably sounds something like:

- Because you're a loser!
- Because you are deluding yourself to think you can really do this!
- Because nobody wants to support the arts!
- Because most artists don't make any money until they're dead!
- Because you totally suck!

Not very empowering, huh?

Why does your mind play such tricks on you? Why does it set you up for failure? Is it just being "realistic"? Or is there a better answer?

(Do you like how I just used four more questions to move this section along?)

You get such negative, deflating answers because your amazing mind is simply responding to the input it was given. A question like "Why can't I get a break?" presupposes that good fortune is indeed eluding you. To keep from fighting with itself, your brain processes it as the truth and then has to justify why this reality exists. The only "right" answers must be negative to support the original input.

Does that make sense?

It's based on an idea you've probably heard before: Crap in = crap out. Quality in = quality out. Mediocre data in = mediocre data out.

Therefore, if you want to be an Empowered Artist, you must learn to ask better questions. But it won't happen on its own. At first you must be purposeful and deliberate with the process.

Left to its own devices, your mind is prone to wander into negativity and fear. So you must train your brain to run more efficiently. To stay with the computer analogy, you have to upgrade to a new and improved operating system.

Here are examples of better questions:

- Even though the local arts scene isn't thriving, what could I do to inject it with excitement?
- What cool event or project could I create that would get attention, help the community, and propel my career?

Now those are powerful questions! They inspire your mind to conjure up expansive ideas and seek out new opportunities. They lead to solutions instead of simply justifying what's wrong. They empower you to take action and improve whatever situation you find yourself in.

Isn't that a much better way to think and live?

Call to Action

It's time to get out your notebook or journal again. Take a pen or pencil and draw a vertical line down the middle of the page. On the left side write down a list of the low-quality questions you ask yourself.

Sometimes these will be literal questions that you articulate (like "Why is this city so lame?"). Other times they will be hidden and you'll need to dig for them. You'll usually find the question intertwined with the dominant thought behind your negative internal dialogue.

For instance, if you often think "I can't find a paying gig to save my life," the underlying question may be "Why is nobody willing to pay me for my talents?"

However you uncover them, write down the most prominent and reoccurring questions that hold you back. Now go back to the top of your list. For every negative question on the left, write a new empowering question on the right.

Examples:

"Why doesn't anyone care about my art?" could be transformed into "Who has been positively impacted by my art" or "What could I do with my next painting that would blow people away?"

The first new question asks you to focus on the positive feedback you have received (even if it's only been from a handful of people). The other question inspires you to think in fresh and expansive ways.

If you wrote "Why am I not selling any of my music?" on the left, you might counter with "What are the top ten things I could do to sell more music this week?" on the right.

Believe me, this exercise is not just rearranging the semantic deck chairs on a sinking ship. This is the type of thought process that leads to action and results in the real world!

So, the next time you catch yourself uttering a self-defeating thought, stop and ask yourself a better, more empowering question.

10) Do the work

I'll do my best to approach this subject without sounding like a nagging parent or a domineering boss. But brace yourself anyway for some stern advice. Even though it's listed at the end of ten foundational principles, this may be the most important aspect of becoming an Empowered Artist.

We've touched on it throughout these early sections (especially in the "Prioritize your art" principle), and we will surely address it again. But this element is so crucial to your success, it deserves special attention here.

To do anything significant with your creativity, you must be willing to do the work! You must spend a considerable amount of time engaged in your chosen craft.

Of course, the "work" I refer to here doesn't have to be a source of drudgery, like many "day jobs" can be. However, like a day job, it should be an activity you immerse yourself in on a regular, preplanned basis.

To put this in the simplest possible terms ... If you are a writer ... write! If you are a painter ... paint! If you are a designer ... design! If you are an actor ... act!

Don't think of your calling as simply a noun or category (such as reggae music, romance novels, or abstract art). To be an Empowered Artist, you must think of your talent as a verb – an activity you engage in consistently.

There are countless people around the world who love to think about being an artist. They love to talk about what they hope to do with their creative skills. They ponder and plan. But the amount of time and energy they put into actually doing the thing is minimal.

Don't be one of these people!

As Anna Deavere Smith, author of *Letters to a Young Artist*, says, "Talking about acting is like thinking about swimming."

You can't wait for the time to be right or for inspiration to strike. You must have regular, consistent blocks of time devoted to doing the important work of creativity. And you must honor and protect that commitment, come rain or come shine, come hell or high water.

Unless you are simply an artistic dabbler (which is fine if you decide that's how creativity fits into your life) then you must make excellence and even mastery your North Star. You may never feel that you arrive at this exalted position, but your ongoing habits should focus on discipline, experimentation and growth.

To prosper and evolve as an artist, you must have a serious work ethic when it comes to your craft. I know, it sounds a lot like a "real job," doesn't it? And the truth is, it may turn out to be the most authentic and realistic job you will ever have.

Call to Action

Now is the time to get totally honest with yourself. Do you really devote enough time to your music, art, writing, photography, or other chosen form of creative expression? Are you seriously doing the work? And, if the answer is yes, are you doing it on a consistent, ongoing basis?

Or, do you get sidetracked easily? Do weeks go by when you either don't feel like creating or it slips your mind? Do you have a long list of excuses for why now is not the right time to fully engage in your art?

Do this: Take a look at how you answered the Call to Action for principle 3, "Prioritize your art." In that one you identified blocks of time that you would "ink" onto your calendar every week. These pre-determined time slots were set aside solely for working on your craft.

(If you didn't complete that exercise, now would be a great time to do it!)

To cement these commitments into your schedule, take this one extra step: Have conversations with the most important people in your life who might distract you from your new creative obligations. These people might include your spouse, significant other, parents, children, close friends, etc.

Let each person know how much they mean to you and how much you value your relationship with them. Then explain your new commitment to feeding your soul's purpose and the need to devote regular, undistracted blocks of time to it. Ask for their assistance in honoring the time and space you have set aside for this purpose.

Ask how you can still meet their needs while tending to your new creative priorities. Let them know you are relying on their support. Make any needed adjustments to your schedule, and post it on a wall or digital calendar where everyone can see it. Then live up to your newfound commitment to "do the work" that's necessary to grow your art.

The Launching Pad: Essential Elements for Kicking Your Art Activities Into Overdrive

1) Find your voice

You know when you see it or hear it. The look, the style, or the sound is instantly recognizable. Most likely, you know a Van Gogh or Picasso painting as soon as you see one. When you hear the guitar and lead vocals, you know it's a song by U2. When those distinct harmonies kick in, you know it's the Beach Boys. The same can be said for Frank Sinatra, the Beatles, Michael Jackson, Celine Dion, and AC/DC.

Likewise, popular writers, poets and authors each have a unique "voice" – Ernest Hemingway, Mark Twain, Elizabeth Gilbert, Maya Angelou, Stephen King, to name a few. No one else on the planet weaves together words quite the same way that he or she does.

I've seen this same element at work even with successful artists who are not household names. Of the hundreds of thriving creative types I've interviewed over the decades, most of them served a niche audience, under the mass media radar. And, nearly all of them had developed a distinct style that their small but supportive fan base had fallen in love with.

One of your goals as an Empowered Artist is to find your voice and signature style. You must discover, through experimentation and prolific output, the unmistakable form of expression that demonstrates who you are.

However, there are four important distinctions that need to be made regarding this topic:

- Do not put too much pressure on yourself to find your voice right away. If you already have a sense of what it is, that's great. But if you have no clue yet, relax. It's okay. Allow plenty of time to discover it. That's one of the reasons you "do the work" on a daily and weekly basis. It helps you hone your craft, sharpen your saw, and organically develop your signature style.

- Most artists are inspired by people they admire. Whether it's your favorite singer, actor or fashion designer ... someone influenced you to pursue your creative path. Your early work was probably a tribute to them – an attempt to recreate their style. And that's a great way to begin.

  But over time, your own voice will emerge. And it's your job to nurture that impulse of individuality, not to be a copy of someone else's style. Let imitation be a starting point and not a destination.

- Don't live in fear of being stuck with a recognizable style. Yes, if you are successful with a unique way of expressing yourself, you will get requests to produce more of it. And you might get bored with it. But if that's your biggest problem, you're pretty damn fortunate.

  At the same time, you can evolve. Add something new to your familiar approach to art. Deliver it in an unexpected way. Morph it into a new medium that you feel called to explore. Also, do your best to grow your art career in a way that brings your existing fans along with you.

- Finally, realize that you can also feature different styles on different projects. Prolific author James Patterson has his Alex Cross series, Michael Bennett series, Women's Murder Club series, as well as a Middle School series, Witch and Wizard series, and more. This allows him to remain consistent and familiar within projects while also exploring new genres.

  Musicians have theme albums, fashion designers have seasonal lines, visual artists have themed shows. You can even have different stylistic phases throughout your career, such as Picasso's "Blue Period." If you crave variety, this may be the way to go.

Call to Action

As I've said, there's no reason to rush the process of defining your voice and personal style, so don't put undue pressure on yourself. However, if you're up for the challenge, it wouldn't hurt to take a stab at it. Perhaps you've already developed an approach to your craft that can be easily described and communicated.

If it helps, here's a formula you can use to get the ball rolling:

I create [a specific type of art] **that make(s)** [a specific type of person] **feel** [a beneficial emotion or feeling].

Examples:

- I create acoustic music that makes stressed-out business people feel relaxed.

- I create family portraits that make parents feel proud.
- I create romantic thrillers that make sophisticated women feel adventurous.
- I create risqué puppet shows that make adults feel like teenagers again.

Of course, the formula can be tweaked and shortened for public consumption, such as:

- Family portraits for proud parents
- Romantic thrillers for sophisticated women

I realize these phrases don't completely sum up the unique way you create your art. Even though it can be instantly recognized, your style isn't always easy to describe. But doing this exercise forces you to think about it and clarify the traits that set you apart.

2) Move your feet

I have several friends and acquaintances who I refer to as "perpetual planners." They love to strategize their impending creative careers. They endlessly read books, do research, attend workshops, create timelines, make lists, plot out scenarios, and brainstorm ideas. Some even produce entire business plans for what they hope to accomplish with their creativity.

But guess what? All of their plans and preparations are missing one key ingredient:

Implementing the ideas they come up with!

I'm sorry, but ideas alone do not empower you. Making lists alone will not help you make progress. Brainstorming alone will not get your art out into the world.

I understand the appeal of being in planning mode. You do need to take some sort of "action" to read and research, to brainstorm and make lists. These activities make people feel like they are doing something, like they are being proactive.

But when the momentum stops there, no real progress is made. The needle doesn't move. The world continues to be robbed of the gifts you have to offer.

There's an African proverb that says, "When you pray, move your feet." At first glance, it seems like it's saying you should dance or move while you pray. What it really means is this: Your desires, hopes and dreams must be coupled with action for them to manifest into physical form.

In the context of the proverb, I think of all the planning that people do as prayers. They are wishes served up to the Universe or to whatever you consider the Almighty to be. They represent your best intentions and aspirations, and they are vitally important to your growth as an artist. But they are merely a starting point.

I met with one of my perpetual planner friends recently. He said, "I'm ready to get serious with my artwork, but I feel stuck. I'd love to brainstorm some ideas with you."

I stopped him, then lovingly said, "You don't need another list, my friend. What's holding you back has nothing to do with needing a new plan or idea. You already have plenty of them. What you must do now is pick one and act on it until it's completed."

That's what I mean by "move your feet." Get your grand visions and checklists out of your head and off of the paper. Move them into the real world. Breathe life into them. Create them, display them, promote them. Then take what you learned from the experience and do it all over again, or pick something else and see it through to completion. That's what Empowered Artists do, and that's what you should do too.

Call to Action

Let's make this short and sweet. Look over the lists you have created.

Consider all of the plans you have pondered related to your artistic skills.

Now, using your intelligence, your intuition or your best guess, pick one thing from these lists. I don't care what the thing is or how you choose it. Heck, for all I care, you can just throw a dart at the list and see where it lands. The main thing is that you decide on a specific course of action.

Have you decided? Great! But you're not done yet. Now take some small action on it. It doesn't matter what the action is. All that matters is that you do it. (However, making another list is strictly off limits!)

Send an email, make a phone call, drive to the gallery, get out your guitar or keyboard, lay out a blank canvas, open up that file of the novel you started months ago.

The size of the action isn't important. In fact, it's better if it's small. That way, you can make sure it gets done. You can celebrate a small victory. Really do this. And do it now.

I'll wait here while you get it done ...

Did you do it? Yes?

Congratulations! You just moved your feet!

3) Crave speed

If you read the previous "Move your feet" principle, you understand the importance of taking action on your plans. Let's hit this topic from another angle that will be equally essential to your success in the arts.

The best way to summarize this is to say, "Empowered Artists love speed." People who thrive in creative fields are not only action oriented, they are also constructively impatient. They are eager to share their music, art and ideas – sooner rather than later.

Artists who struggle tend to hesitate. They convince themselves that there are all sort of reasons why they must wait before they step into their greatness. The time isn't right. The economy is bad. The information they require isn't available yet.

All of these distractions and delays are cleverly disguised as sound reasons to keep you from taking action. Using fear and uncertainly as a backdrop, they lure you into a sense of relief and comfort, like a rest stop along the highway.

They hypnotically whisper, "It's nice and comfortable here. We have complimentary excuses you can use to justify why you need to wait. Plus, you'll get free back rubs and foot massages. You can get back on the road later. We promise ... later."

I admit, it's appealing. But, I emphatically ask you: Why do you need to rest, when you haven't even started the real journey yet? Would you pack up your car to go on a vacation, and then one block down the road pull over at a rest stop? Of course not! Stopping so soon would only ensure that you don't go anywhere.

So make a commitment to go somewhere. Fall in love with speed. Don't excessively ponder, don't over plan, don't delay. Start your creative journey today!

Call to Action

Okay, allow me to play devil's advocate for a moment. You literally can't do everything you want to do. You shouldn't act on every random thought that pops into your mind. That would make your life pretty chaotic.

But you can and should be doing something, and the time to do that specific thing is now. The trick is deciding what that thing is.

For me, it all starts with the craft itself. As I've said before, Empowered Artists put a priority on honing their skills and spend liberal amounts of time doing the work of creation. So, the best action you can take every day is to write, paint, sing, design, dance, etc.

Beyond that, what is the most important and exciting next step? What holds the greatest potential for reaching new fans, expanding your network, or generating income? What feels like it would be the most enjoyable and creatively satisfying?

Decide what that next step is. Perhaps it's the action you chose in the previous section, or maybe it's something else. Whatever it is, pick it. Then – you guessed it – do something about it.

If you have set a goal to write a book, the time to start writing it is NOW. If you have decided to record a new music album, the time to start writing and recording is NOW. If you have chosen the theme of your next visual art series, the time to start painting is NOW.

With rare exceptions, the answer to the question "When?" is always "NOW!"

4) Get into alignment

In an earlier section called "Know your mode" we covered the imbalance someone can feel when they mentally think they are in one career mode while their actions reflect a different direction. (Remember the eagle and the jackhammer exercise?)

Let's hit this concept on an even deeper level to reveal another trait that will build your empowerment muscles. Someday I may write an entire book on this topic, but for now let me summarize the principle. To be a fully functioning Empowered Artist (and human being), you must be in alignment in four distinct areas:

- What you think
- What you feel
- What you say
- What you do

If one or more of these aspects fight with your true ambitions, you'll feel conflicted and your progress will be slow.

To clarify, let's quickly break down these four elements:

What you think – Obviously, this refers to your thoughts, including everything from random mind chatter to purposeful planning and affirmations.

What you feel – This includes your emotions, which can be described with words such as happy, content, proud, nervous, excited, fearful, sad, and more.

What you say – This element encompasses what you say out loud, both to yourself and to others.

What you do – You should know this one by now – it's the actions you take, the behaviors you exhibit in the physical world.

I'm sure you know where I'm going with this, but let's examine it anyway. Can you think of situations in your life where you went in one direction with two or three of the elements, but veered in an opposing direction with other elements?

For instance, perhaps you told people about your new art project and read statements every day that affirmed your desire to make it happen. Emotionally, you were quite excited about it. But ... not a lot happened with the actual "work" of getting it done. Therefore, the project was never completed.

Another example: Maybe you made plans to record a new music album, visualized your success, made grand plans, and even spent a lot of time in the recording studio. At the same time, you were afraid and felt like a fraud. You muttered things to yourself and your friends like, "No one is buying music anymore. Why am I killing myself over this? At least my CDs will make nice coasters some day."

Can you see the internal conflicts this misalignment can cause?

Empowered Artists do everything in their power to be fully integrated. They strive to have all four aspects (thoughts, feelings, words, and deeds) moving in the same direction. When you reach this state of alignment, you have power. You become unstoppable.

Call to Action

Perhaps you're worried and thinking to yourself, "Oh no, I do this misalignment thing all the time. I'm doomed." If that's the case, here's my advice: Relax!

Few human beings are in balance with all four elements at all times. We all have our moments. We all have doubts and fears. There are times when words slip out and actions don't get taken as we had planned. When you find yourself misfiring, don't beat yourself up. Just be aware.

And that's your homework with this section. Be present with what you think, feel, say and do as often as you can. The first step toward alignment is monitoring how you juggle the four elements. Most people walk through their lives asleep – completely clueless about how they operate.

But you can be different. You can be more conscious of the choices you make, the emotions you feel, and the actions you take. Soon you will catch yourself being out of sync and will make quick adjustments. Like any new skill, it takes time and practice to get good at it. But I guarantee, it's worth the effort.

5) Know that you're not broken

This would be a good time to pause and remind you of something important. As we cover the many principles of becoming an Empowered Artist, this alarming thought might enter your mind:

"Holy crap! I'm doing so many things wrong. I really need to get my act together!"

If that has occurred to you, congratulations! That means you're gaining insights and are ready for growth. That means you are serious about taking your art to a new level of prominence.

At the same time, I want to remind you of this:

You are not broken. You are not damaged goods. Just because you are not where you want to be, YOU – personally – are not a failure. You have simply done what you thought was best up until this point in your life.

If you see a lot of areas where you need to make adjustments, that's okay. Who doesn't have room for improvement? So don't label yourself as faulty or defective. As my friend Jami Lula sings, "You're perfect. You're golden."

So many people spend their lives trying to fix what's wrong with them. They read books, attend workshops, immerse themselves in multi-week programs, and even have psychic readings ... all in an attempt to mend the cracks in their lives. But what they do is equate the blemishes in certain areas of their life with their entire worth as a person.

If this describes you, please stop! You are who you are and that's enough. You're wonderful just as you are. You are a unique expression of the miraculous intelligence that created the Great Orion nebula, the Grand Canyon, and Monster Truck shows. (I was hoping to make you laugh. This was getting way too serious.)

Your job isn't to repair yourself. Your real mission is to discover who you are and then express that fully and authentically.

Rev. Michael Beckwith said it best when he implored, "Stop trying to fix yourself. Start to be yourself!"

I can't say it any better than that.

Call to Action

Before I give you a suggested action step, I want to clarify: There's nothing wrong with reading books, attending workshops, and enrolling in programs. (Heck, even psychic readings can be fun.) As long as you're doing them for the right reasons.

Yes, you need to improve your craft. Yes, you need to be constantly learning and growing. Yes, a certain amount of "constructive discontent" can be valuable.

But if you're trying to cure yourself of being a flawed human being, that needs to stop. If the action is supposed to "fix" a broken you (instead of improve a behavior like planning, productivity, or technical skills), slow down.

Another way to put this: Separate the trait you want to improve from your overall sense of worth as a person and an artist. You're not repairing damaged goods, you're improving upon the great raw material that is already there.

The next time you think about buying a book, attending a class, or doing any other personal transformation work, ask these two questions:

- Will this help me discover who I truly am?
- Will it help me more fully express myself?

If the answers are yes, then it's probably worth doing. Otherwise, you may be operating from "I need fixing" mode.

But, as I hope you now know, you're not broken. You don't need to be fixed. You just need to uncover the real you, polish it up a bit, and let it shine.

6) Get friendly with money

Money is right up there with politics, religion, and sex on the list of subjects that carry heaps of emotional baggage. There are so many stigmas and associations attached to this topic, especially when you mix commerce with art, I don't even know where to start.

Some people buy into the "starving artist" concept or feel that money somehow taints their craft. Others want to make money but feel that "selling" art lowers their integrity or causes them to "sell out."

Whew. I'm getting a headache just thinking about all these disgraceful attachments.

So let's begin here:

If you harbor any negative associations with making money from your talents ... *get over it!* (Was that too abrupt?)

Seriously, why do creative people make it such a burden to generate cash flow? Why is covering your expenses, making some extra money, or even earning a living from art so difficult to pursue? Why is it so painful?

I'm not even talking about the pain of bringing in lower amounts of money than you had hoped for. (Yes, that can hurt.) I'm just talking about the pain of mentally wrestling with the subject. The agony of learning how to sell, the fear of being perceived as greedy, the anguish of having to promote your work and ask for the sale.

You might as well back up the Piles of Pain dump truck and deposit it right there at your feet. Geez!

I suggest you take Nancy Reagan's advice and "Just say no!" (If you were born after 1980, don't worry about that reference.)

Here's the lowdown: You need money to survive. You need money to feel secure and take care of yourself and your family. You need money to be able to help others and make a bigger impact in the world. Money allows you to focus more on your art and honing your craft, as opposed to spending most of your time working to pay the bills.

Do you think a plumber or electrician is "greedy" if they ask for money? What about someone who starts a restaurant? Are they tainted if they charge for the food they prepare and serve? Of course not. A restaurant owner does the important work of feeding people's stomachs. Artists do the work of feeding people's souls – which is just as important and valuable.

Make no mistake: Money is good and good for you! Please get this through your head. Relieve yourself of the negative associations and stigmas. Dump your money baggage at the door, or better yet, kick it to the curb to be picked up and taken away on trash day.

Call to action

Do you want to know what the main mental culprit is when it comes to the struggles that artists have with money? It's the belief that making money is a win-lose proposition. The logic (or illogic) goes something like this:

If I "talk someone out of" their money in exchange for my (art, music, book, film, etc.), I win and they lose. I have just successfully taken their money from them.

Hooray for me! I have now proven myself to be a manipulating, greedy bastard!

But is that true? Of course not!

The real truth is that making money is an "exchange" of value. The fan or customer spends their money so they can receive something of great worth in return. The value for them is an experience, a feeling, a thrill, or some other sense of satisfaction.

I'll go even further than that and say that it should not be an "even exchange" of value at all. When delivered in the right manner, the value your paying customer receives will be worth much more than the money they had to part with to get it.

Can you see how much of a positive influence this line of thinking could have on your relationship with money and art? It transforms you from being a taker to being a giver. And that's a much better place to be.

Your homework is to repeat this affirmation to yourself:

"My art delivers great value to the people who truly resonate with me and my offerings. My talents and creative output have the potential to enhance the lives of many people. In exchange for delivering that value, I deserve to be well compensated.

"I will be a good steward of the money I earn and will use it to cover my living expenses, reward myself for the good work I do, and invest it to make even more art in the future. Money is good, and I look forward to the flow of more of it into my life."

7) Have a structure in place

Here's another element you'll need to grow your creative career, especially if cultivating fans and generating revenue are part of your plan.

It's related to a common problem I've seen with countless artists. The good people affected by it are talented and well-meaning. They do great work and are devoted to their craft. But they are also plagued by low sales and minimal cash flow. They hone their skills and maybe even share their art with people, but the response is lackluster.

When I take a closer look at their activities, I can often spot the problem right away: There's no specific structure in place that gives people a clear way to support their art.

It's one thing to create and even display or perform your art (both online and in physical spaces). It's quite another to offer specific ways that new and existing fans can experience your craft and pay you.

For instance, I know many musicians who perform live at various venues and sell original music CDs and downloads. Many of them are quite good, but many also complain about few gigs and slow sales.

When someone asks these artists what they do, they give generic answers about playing around town and writing their own music.

Then there are musicians like Shannon Curtis. If you ask her what she does, she'll tell you that she is a singer-songwriter who specializes in house concert tours and writing personalized original songs for people to give as gifts for special occasions.

Shannon rarely performs at traditional venues any more. Nearly all of her live shows are done in homes, organized by her many fans, who gather 20 or more of their friends for these private concerts. She does about 60 of these house concerts every summer.

She has CDs and merchandise for sale, available in various bundled packages. And she offers the personal song service for fees ranging from $500 to $2,000.

That's what she does, and that's how you can enjoy her music and support her.

But most artists aren't that clear. They do a little of this and a little of that. They meander and follow their muse. Then they leave it up to potential fans to figure out what the artist really does and what he or she has to offer.

To be an Empowered Artist, you must have a structure in place – a clear way for people to play with you, support you, and pay you.

Take a look at your current efforts. Do you give people clear choices? Or are you all over the map? When you answer the question, "So what do you do?" ... are you focused or fuzzy?

You'll make a lot more progress if you offer clear choices and a solid structure.

Call to action

Here's an easy way to solve this weak structure dilemma. Pick three main things that you will offer for sale to the public. Even if you have a wide array of interests and skills and hate to be pigeonholed, just humor me and pick three.

Also, make sure these offerings are at three different price points: low, medium, and high. Don't make the mistake of only selling low-priced art in an attempt to reach more people or make it more affordable for the struggling masses. Give people who have disposable income a way to support you and benefit from your talent too.

Some examples:

- A musician might offer a $15 CD, a $75 bundle of music and merchandise, and a $500 private concert package.

- A nonfiction author could offer a $20 book, a $97 online course, and a $1,000 one-on-one coaching program.

- A visual artist might charge $25 for prints, $500 for original paintings, and $2,000 for a wall mural.

Of course, you can create things outside of these three strict categories, and you can change your public offers as you evolve as an artist. But making things clear for potential buyers like this will go a long way to improving your impact and income.

8) Tune into your fan frequency

Some people call them customers or clients. Some call them patrons or supporters. I like to call them fans. These are the good people who fall in love with your creative work and, in the process of getting to know you, fall in love with you.

You need fans. You want fans — and lots of them. Of all the factors that influence an artist's success, nothing trumps having a large and enthusiastic fan base. That's why for decades my mantra to creative people has consistently been "focus on fans."

Don't get overly obsessed with impressing industry gatekeepers, such as gallery owners, magazine editors, talent buyers, agents, managers, etc. None of those people will matter if you can't build a fan base of individuals who support you.

Great. But as you set out on your quest to attract fans, you'll quickly find that most people don't seem to give a damn. They barely notice you. And, if you do catch their eye, they rapidly move on to the next shiny object.

Empowered Artists accept this reality and brace themselves for it. Sure, it can be a little painful at first, but they learn to accept that not everyone is going to resonate with their heartfelt creations. In fact, MOST people will not be interested at all.

But that's okay, because your goal is not to please everyone. You can't possibly win over the general population. So don't even try. That's a sure recipe for chronic frustration.

Your new goal is to think like a tuning fork.

Did you know that if you hit one tuning fork and get it vibrating, then place another non-vibrating tuning fork next to it, the second fork will begin to vibrate at the same frequency?

It does that because the sound waves of the first tuning fork resonate with the second one, causing them to vibrate in sync with each other, even if no one touches the second tuning fork.

If you placed a sock or a banana next to the first tuning fork, it would not noticeably respond at all. It wouldn't resonate with the tuning fork.

What a great analogy for connecting with your ideal fans!

Your job from here on out is to simply put out a specific creative and stylistic vibration of sorts. Then pay attention to who resonates with it. Most people will be like socks and bananas; they won't be in sync with your vibe. But you'll soon discover that people who occupy a certain slice of the population will perk up and vibrate right along with you.

These are your ideal fans. These are the people you want to serve and cater to and heap praise upon. These are the people who matter most in your creative life.

So, when you find those precious beings who resonate with you, cultivate relationships with them. Thank them, appreciate them, and love them.

Bottom line: The height of your career in the arts will be determined by the relationships you build with your ideal fans.

Call to action

As I mentioned before, this book will not delve very deeply into marketing. I have created many other resources on that topic over the years and I suggest you consult those titles for in-depth marketing advice.

But we will flirt with promotion and sales ideas a bit throughout these pages. This exercise does just that.

If you're sold on the tuning fork analogy, it would be helpful to start clarifying just who these resonating people are. As you build a fan base, you will start to notice some commonalities and patterns among the good people who support you. Of course, they won't all be cookie-cutter versions of each other, but you should find some overlapping traits.

Take a few minutes and write out a profile of the type of person who would tend to like you and spend money on your unique form of talent. Your goal is to describe the kind of individual who is predisposed to like what you offer. In other words, something about them makes them more likely than not to resonate with the creative vibration you emit into the world.

Two big factors to start with are age and gender. How old do your fans tend to be? Are they primarily men or women? Then consider a range of other factors: where they work, what they do for fun, where they hang out and shop, how they get information.

Also ask: What is their overall mindset? Which way do they lean politically, spiritually, and socially? What causes do they support? What makes them tick?

Creating a profile of your ideal fan in this way will help you find more people who resonate with you as you grow your creative career.

9) Enlist the twin soldiers

When it comes to having a thriving, long-term career in the arts, this is the element that has the biggest impact. I've seen it used by most of the truly successful musicians, authors, and artists I've interviewed over the decades. It has also been the difference maker in my own self-employment journey in the arts.

I call them the "twin soldiers," not because I like military references, but because I think of them as steadily marching on through the battles and the victories of a creative life.

Allow me to introduce you to Consistency and Repetition.

Yes, they are related, but they also serve separate functions. If you can learn to make them a part of who you are, your life and art will be served well.

Think about the creative people you know and support. Make a list of the writers, designers, performers, and artists whose work touches your heart and frequently comes to mind. Most likely, they didn't just start creating last week.

I'll wager that you've known about these artists for some time. Or, if you only recently discovered them, they have been plying their craft for many years. Really think about the creative people you admire. How long have they been sharing their gifts with the public? How consistent have they been with their style and approach?

I think your answers will support my twin soldiers premise: The most successful artists employ consistency and repetition over time. For the most part, they're not in and out of the marketplace. They don't dabble and create when they can get around to it. They generally don't disappear for long periods of time.

They have a consistent style and attitude (even though they do evolve as artists over time) and they stay at it, repeatedly, for years on end.

That's exactly how I build my career and identity as an author, speaker and teacher. By doggedly cranking out articles, blog posts, podcasts, and video clips, while also doing interviews and presenting live workshops. I've been at it pretty much nonstop for nearly 25 years.

Look at the consistent output from fiction writers such as Nora Roberts, Janet Evanovich, Neil Gaiman, and Dean Koontz. Think about the ongoing activities of Beyonce, Taylor Swift, and the Rolling Stones. Look at any creative field and you'll find similar examples of successful artists staying active and visible for years on end.

Yes, it's a grind. And that's what separates the pros from the wannabe's. Pros are willing to grind it out – consistently and repeatedly – over time.

I must point out that creating and promoting your art consistently does not guarantee monetary success. There are too many other variables that can influence your ultimate results. But without consistency and repetition, you are almost assured of not reaching your full potential.

So send your twin soldiers to boot camp. Whip them into shape. Then give them marching orders and put them to work building your legacy in the arts.

Call to action

As I wrote in earlier sections, you don't have to strive for full-time status to be an Empowered Artist. If you're simply in it to express yourself through a sideline venture, that's great, and you can go easy on this twin soldiers idea.

But if you have any inkling at all to build a career and make a long-term impact with your art, I encourage you to embrace consistency and repetition.

Since you're already committed to honing your craft and have blocked out time on your calendar for creating (you did do those things, right?), this is a good time for another affirmation.

Read this to yourself to ingrain the philosophy:

"I know my art is valuable and will touch thousands of lives as I connect with my ideal fans. The best way to grow as an artist and extend my reach is to be consistent with how I show up in the world. I now commit to having an ongoing presence in the places where my ideal fans hang out.

"I am willing, able and eager to grind it out and repeatedly get my work out into the marketplace, for months and years on end, no matter what is going on in the world or in my life. This is not simply something I do; it's an essential part of who I am as an artist."

Creativity Career Killers: The Top Ten Misguided Notions That May Be Holding You Back

1) Lack of time

Artists face a lot of obstacles along the road to pursuing their dreams. These hurdles come in all shapes and sizes – from big and ugly to little and annoying. But there's one thing I can say with certainty about these creative roadblocks:

Almost all of them are self-imposed.

Yep. No matter how much you want to blame something "out there" for your troubles, with rare exception, the obstacles you face are self-made. They are sad stories you tell yourself about the world that you fervently treat as the Gospel truth. And these epic tales are blurring your vision and keeping you from making progress with your art.

In this section we'll cover ten nasty creativity career killers, starting with this perennial classic:

"I don't have time to devote to my art!"

Really? You don't have time? Did you get shortchanged when the Laws of Physics Gods were doling out 24-hour days? "Hey, I only got a 17-hour day! What gives?"

Here's the thing about time:

It's the true equalizer. It's one of the only things that is evenly distributed among all human beings. You can make a rational argument that some people have more money, better looks, a fatter

Rolodex, nicer cars, and so on. But everyone gets the exact same amount of time to work with.

I know, you have to work or you have kids or you take care of aging parents. Yes, there are life obligations that appear to suck up most of our time and keep us from doing the things we truly love. But is that truly an accurate assessment of your situation?

In the early years of building my reputation and body of work as an author, I had a lot of constraints. I worked a full-time job, my daughter was a toddler, and I was recovering from a divorce. I also played in a band and acted in a couple of plays every year.

I could have easily told myself I didn't have the time to devote to writing books and marketing my work on this new thing called the Internet. But I resisted that seductive story and, instead, carved out time here and there when I could.

Even if I had only a few minutes to spare, I would make time to tweak a book outline, flesh out an article, or interact in an online forum. I chipped away at the things that needed to be done, while also handling all of my other responsibilities the best I could.

Was it easy? No. Did I whine and complain? Sometimes. Was it worth it? Absolutely! One thing I have never uttered to myself is, "I wish I had started doing this creative stuff later." No one who puts in the effort to do something worthy regrets it, and you won't either.

The truth is, you'll never have "more time." Something will always come along to fill the void. So stop deluding yourself that now is not a good time to devote to your art. You can decide right now that your creativity is important, and that you'll find the time to invest in it.

You may be thinking, "This guy just doesn't know my schedule and list of obligations." The truth is, I do. I juggle a ton of stuff in my own life. At times it can seem overwhelming. I'm not denying that.

I'm also not suggesting that you should pack every waking minute with activity. You also need to carve out time for rest and self care. As always, your goal should be equilibrium and balance. And, if you accept your role as an Empowered Artist, you'll also make time for your art. The good news is, doing it can be a lot easier than you think.

Call to action

When Jerry Seinfeld was an up-and-coming comedian, he made a commitment to write one joke a day. Not an entire routine or monologue. Just one funny line. He had a big calendar of the whole year on a wall in his apartment. Every time he wrote a joke, he put a red X on that date. Before long he had a growing chain of red X's on the calendar – a visual reminder of the consistent work he put in.

Seinfeld once shared the story of his calendar and the chain of red X's with a young comic. His main advice: Don't break the chain! Do something related to your craft every day, no matter how small the action is.

This idea dovetails perfectly with "tiny habits," a popular concept that's been making the rounds in recent years. Using this approach, you commit to taking one small action every day toward a bigger habit you want to develop. For instance, if you want to run a marathon, you would simply commit to running ten yards today. That's all. Then run ten yards again tomorrow, and the next day, etc. Even in the freezing cold of winter, someone could run ten yards every day. Easy.

And that's your homework for this principle: Commit to doing your art or music or writing every single day. No exceptions. Even if it's for just five minutes. Seriously. If you're really tired tomorrow and don't feel like doing it, take five minutes and do it anyway. Get out the sketchpad, pick up the guitar, open the file of the book you're working on. Spend a few minutes engaged in your craft.

If you end up spending more time on it (and you often will), great. But at the very least, follow through on your five-minute commitment. And do it every day. I mean it. EVERY DAY! I guarantee, this tiny habit will gain momentum and expand. You'll soon discover there is more time than you previously thought to devote to your art on a daily basis.

If you really want to cement this practice, buy an annual wall calendar like Jerry Seinfeld did. Mark off each day that you lived up to your time commitment. Watch your chain of red X's grow.

And then don't break the chain!

2) Lack of money

Here's another classic excuse that artist's use all the time. Do any of these sound familiar?

- "I'd do a lot more with my art if I had more money to invest in it."
- "It takes money to make money."
- "Sure, she's doing great with her art. She must be a trust-fund baby or have a sugar daddy on the side."

I could list a lot more worn-out phrases like this, but I'll spare you the agony. Which begs the question: Do you spare yourself the agony that comes with carrying this "lack of money" baggage around with you?

Okay, let's first deal with the realities:

I admit that some full-time creative people have built-in advantages. Maybe their spouse has a cushy job that allows them to focus on art without worrying about paying the bills. Maybe they inherited money or made some smart investments when they were young. Sure, people in those situations exist, so let's acknowledge that and wish them well.

But if you think that's the story behind all of the successful independent artists out there (and there are many of them operating over and under the media radar), you are sadly mistaken. Most people who succeed as musicians, writers, and artists start with very little. They work day jobs and do sideline gigs to pay the bills while they hone their craft and grow a fan base.

I can also tell you with certainty that having money available to spend on your creative pursuits does not automatically lead to success. Not by a long shot. I've watched many people invest tens of thousands of dollars into their careers only to fall flat in the end. There are many factors and variables that go into building a thriving arts career, and having a surplus of money is pretty low on the list.

What's most important is dedicating the time to your craft, breaking through the mental barriers that hold you back, and learning to promote and sell your work to the public. Doing those things consistently over time will produce much bigger results than simply throwing money at your perceived shortcomings.

Call to action

When it comes to money (especially when there's a lack of it to invest), the ideal course of action is to do what you do best: be creative!

I lived the early decades of my life with slim amounts of disposable income. Because of that, I learned to reframe my financial situation. If you are currently low on extra funds, you can view it as a curse or as a gift. I chose to see it as a gift.

Honestly, if you had a lot of money to invest in your art, you'd probably get lazy. You'd end up wasting most of your cash on schemes that would produce no real and lasting results. I know, because I've seen it first hand with friends and clients who I warned ahead of time. But they had to learn for themselves. Fancy press kits and high-priced publicists will only do so much. Most people have unrealistic expectations about their potential return on these investments.

However, when cash is scarce, you get to play. You get to challenge yourself to come up with ideas that will get the job done, regardless of available funds. You get to experiment. That's right, you get to be creative!

And that's your assignment. Make a list of the art you want to produce and the things you want to accomplish with it. Next, brainstorm ideas you can implement that require little or no money at all. How could you use your brains instead of your bank account?

How could you get the materials and equipment you need? How could you promote your next event guerrilla style? How could you attract an audience in a creative, unexpected way?

In other words, when it comes to money, think less like a banker and more like an artist. Because, after all, that's who you are.

3) Lack of connections

I'm sure you've heard this one: "It's not what you know, it's WHO you know that matters." The idea behind this old chestnut is that you must be well connected to the power brokers in your field to have any chance of succeeding with your art.

Let's face it, there is some truth to this. The more people you know who are involved in your line of creative work, the more opportunities you'll have. You could also flip that idea around and update the old phrase above to read "It's not who you know, it's who knows YOU that matters."

Yes, having a circle of creative connections is important. And most artists realize that – which is why so many get frustrated when they feel they're on the outside of some exclusive club. Gallery owners won't return your call. Media people are too distracted to view your press kit. Talent buyers don't seem to give a rat's buttocks.

"Why bother?" you say. "I don't know the secret handshake and I never got the secret decoder ring." So you imagine outlandish conspiracy theories and mumble something about the old boys club.

Let me ask you: Is this how an Empowered Artist thinks and acts? You know the answer: Absolutely not!

An Empowered Artist embraces a balanced perspective. She realizes the importance of building a network of friends, fans, and partners in her creative field. But she also understands that, at the start, most people will be indifferent. Most people involved in the arts are busy.

They're often overworked and underpaid. They have good intentions, but they don't have the mental bandwidth to cater to everyone's needs.

Empowered Artists put themselves in the shoes of the people they are wanting to connect with. They respect the contact's time and busy schedule. They know it will most likely take time for each person to become familiar with who they are and what they do. They accept that their initial outreach will merely pave the way for more productive interactions in the future.

Empowered Artists are patient. They know they are in this creative game for the long haul.

So, don't be an "I don't have the connections" excuse maker. Realize that everyone – including those "lucky" artists who are currently in the spotlight – started out with no connections. No one knew who they were years ago. But over time, their work and their efforts were recognized. Doors slowly opened. Their emails got favorable replies. Opportunities came their way with more regularity.

That's what Empowered Artists do. They relax and allow time to meet people and build fruitful, two-way relationships. And that's what you should do to build your own network of people connections.

Call to action

Your first bit of homework with this section is to stop thinking of venues, galleries, magazines, retail stores, and blogs as mechanical entities. They are not Cybermen from a *Doctor Who* episode. These entities exist because there is a person (or group of people) behind them. Your mission is not to contact "the gallery." Your goal is to start a relationship with a specific person at the gallery.

Once you've got this people-focused perspective firmly ingrained, compile a sensible list of the places and media outlets you want to connect with. Then do some quick research to uncover a specific name of the best person to contact at each place. Call the store, visit the website, do whatever it takes to get the name, as well as the person's email address and/or direct phone number.

Finally, make your first attempt to contact them. But – and this is important – don't ask for anything with this initial message. Pay them a compliment. Thank them for the work they do. Briefly introduce yourself and let them know you will get back to them soon with a project you are working on. Ask them any questions you have about submission requirements, what they're looking for, etc.

Take these simple steps. Stay in touch and follow up with these people. Be pleasantly persistent, dependable, and easy to work with. Then repeat the process all over again with another group of people you want to get to know. Before you know it, you'll be "well connected."

4) Lack of experience

This creativity career killer is typically used when someone is in the early stages of developing their artistic skills. The person feels they aren't ready to share their gifts with the world. It's too soon. They feel they need to wait until they know more, get better at their craft, feel more confident, and on and on.

A certain degree of this mindset is valid. It usually wouldn't be wise to contact the premier venue in town if you've never displayed your art outside of your basement. Even though there are exceptions, the best approach is to start with smaller venues and slowly work your way up the food chain. This way, your confidence and skills grow along with the level of exposure you earn.

The problem is that a lot of creative people use this "I don't have enough experience yet" scapegoat long after their novice days are behind them. I've seen truly gifted and prolific musicians, writers and artists hold themselves back using this flimsy justification.

Many artists feel they don't yet know enough about the business, best practices, proper protocols, etc. And it doesn't help that there are many experts out there who scare creative people into thinking that they need to be ultra prepared before they venture into the jungle of building a career. Frankly, I think this advice is inflated and overrated.

Years ago the guitar player in my band called to tell me that he had just left a voice mail message on the comment line of a local TV station. Our band had a new CD coming out and he thought it would be cool if we played live during the station's morning news show.

I praised my band mate for taking action. But I also laughed and explained how using a public comment line was not a very effective way to contact the media. I told him he'd be lucky if anyone even heard his message and to not get his hopes up.

An hour later he called back to say that a producer from the station had just called him and asked if our band could play live on the air in two weeks. I was stunned. After all, I was the "music marketing expert" with extended knowledge about these things. I was convinced that his primitive approach would fail.

Boy, was that ever a lesson in humility.

Over the years I've come to realize that NOT knowing all the rules is often a blessing. When you're naive and don't know any better, you're more willing to try things and experiment.

I learned this lesson again several years ago when I created some handmade art journals. I didn't know anything about dealing with gift stores, but it seemed like they'd be good places to sell them. I went into the closest gift store near my house and asked for the owner. I showed her my journals and she bought a dozen of them on the spot. I was surprised how easy it was.

When I shared this story with a friend who was experienced at making and selling crafts, she was shocked. Artists usually don't have that type of quick success. There are strict rules to follow, and most shops will only take new items on consignment, not buy them outright like my store owner did.

It was another confirmation that "knowing it all" or having lots of experience isn't all it's cracked up to be. Sometimes, having a beginner's blind enthusiasm can be a great advantage. I hope these stories convince you to get over the "lack of experience" hurdle.

Call to action

As I wrote earlier, if you are truly just starting out, it probably makes sense to set your sights on an easily attainable goal. No matter what your creative field, I'm sure there are many opportunities (both locally and online) that are appropriate for artists at your career stage.

If you're a visual artist, search for CFA's (calls for artists) in your area. If you're a musician, look for venues that have open mic nights. If you're a writer, look for writers groups that present readings and critiques. If you're a playwright, find a community theater group that might present a reading of your play.

If you can't find any existing groups or events in your area, consider starting one yourself. If you were the organizer of an open mic, art show or writers group, you'd get your work out into the world and meet a lot of new people in the process.

Bottom line: Don't wait for experience. Go out and get it by being proactive. And if you are new to your field, take advantage of your beginner's mind. That could very well be the best thing you have going for you!

5) Lack of inspiration

Most of the lack-based obstacles we've covered thus far in this section have been somewhat tangible. You can measure exactly how much time and money you have. And even though the amount of connections and experience you have are more subjective, they are at least somewhat quantifiable. You can wrap your brain around them.

But, when we talk about inspiration, we're dealing with an intangible realm – one that delves into your feelings and even the depths of your soul. But knowing that doesn't make it any less real. This career killer takes many forms that appear to be quite solid and impenetrable.

For instance, how many times have you faced these monsters?

- "I'm just not feeling inspired enough to work on my art today."
- "I'm waiting for the muse (or the Universe, or the spirit of Aunt Gertrude, or the Easter Bunny) to give me a sign that it's time to create."

I think of this as "conditional creativity." Artistic output can't take place until certain conditions are met. Either your workspace has to be clean, or the house needs to be quiet, or all of the chores need to be completed, or you must feel giddy with enthusiasm before you can start.

Wow. Those are a lot of prerequisites to check off before you can sit down to work on your craft. And requiring inspiration to hit you first is one of the most challenging obstacles of all.

E.B. White said it best when he wrote, "A writer who waits for ideal conditions under which to work will die without putting a word on paper." Harsh words, but true.

Luckily, I was weaned off of this inspiration distraction early on. Throughout the ten years I published my music magazine I had to deal with monthly deadlines. I often procrastinated on writing most of the articles until the final days before deadline.

I had advertisers and readers counting on me to deliver by the promised street date, so I had some built-in pressure to get the work done. Did I feel inspired to write during those deadline days? Usually not. Was I excited to start each new article? Sometimes, yes; but often, no.

But I did what every full-fledged artist does: I sat down and began the work of creation. At first, the words came slowly. My pace and concentration were sluggish. I thought of a hundred other things I'd rather be doing. But at some point in the process of typing out the words, I came up with a sentence I liked. That triggered an idea for a new opening or a fresh angle I could take with the article.

Before long, I wasn't forcing myself to write the damn thing. It was flowing from me. I was engaged. I lost track of where I was and how much time was passing. In a funny way (which I know many artists will understand), I was no longer writing the article; I became the article, and it was writing itself.

Yes, I was inspired. The muse was in full force. But I didn't wait for it to show up. I primed the pump and created the perfect environment for it to spring to life.

To hammer home this idea, here's a quote from painter and photographer Chuck Close:

"Inspiration is for amateurs – the rest of us just show up and get to work."

Call to action

When you wait for the muse (aka inspiration) to arrive before you take action, you're putting the mental and emotional elements before the physical and behavioral elements.

Thinking about something before you do it is, of course, the way all material things come into existence. Therefore, placing thoughts before actions can be a powerful combination. You visualize, affirm, plot and plan ... which inspires the necessary actions to bring your ideas to life.

But it works the other way around too. Taking action, especially when you're not in the mood or have no concrete ideas, can lead to flow and inspiration. It's the artist's version of "fake it till you make it." Physical activity does indeed affect your state of mind, and vice versa. They feed off of each other.

The great composer Tchaikovsky once said, "A self-respecting artist must not fold his hands on the pretext that he is not in the mood."

So, your assignment is to live up to the advice I've given a number of times throughout this book. Carve out a time to work on your craft every day. Even if you only have a few minutes, do the creative activity consistently and don't "break the chain."

Also, realize that when people say, "I don't feel inspired," what they really mean is, "I don't have the energy right now to devote to this." One easy solution is to move. Take a walk, do some deep breathing, crank up some disco music and dance. Get your heart pumping and your blood flowing.

Then go work on your art. Before you know it, you'll be in the zone. And, even if the session ends up not being your most inspired, at least you will have lived up to your commitment to your art and to yourself. And you'll be a better, more Empowered Artist because of it.

6) The "right time" trap

Now that we've covered five lack-based creativity career killers, let's turn our attention to five traps that may be holding you back. This first one involves the stories you tell yourself about timing and your justifications for delays.

Do you find yourself putting off your music, art or writing activities until the "right time"? Are you prone to convincing yourself that the ideal situation is right around the corner? It amazes me how resourceful people can be when they need to rationalize avoidance.

Do any of these statements ring a bell?

- "I'll get serious about my art as soon as this semester is over."
- "Man, the holidays are such a busy time, I'll put songwriting on the back burner until January."
- "I'll start writing my book after the big community project I volunteered for is completed."

Whether you know it or not, it takes time and energy to come up with these shallow justifications. Your mind has to work hard to present a convincing case to your internal artist jury. Then you have to make a decision, which becomes easier with the deceptive appeal of inaction.

Why not take the same energy you use to avoid your craft and apply it to actually making art, music, words, and more?

The truth is, "someday soon" and the "right time" rarely come. This mystical state of being is a fantasy circumstance created in your mind. You have a better chance of capturing the Tooth Fairy than you have of arriving at the "right time" to get serious about your art.

So, on one hand, congratulate yourself on crafting this mythical scenario and believing it to be true. What an imagination you have! That will come in handy when you write that epic novel on a future utopian society. But when it comes to honing and sharing your gifts in the real world, these fairy tale validations only stunt your growth and delay your progress.

Here's a new story I encourage you to sell to yourself and believe in:

Once upon a time there was a group of artists. They were searching for the best time to start working consistently on their various creative skills. They traveled many miles to visit the wisest wizard in all the land. They begged him for his sage wisdom.

He pronounced onto them, "The best time to get started with your creative project is NOW! The best time to continue moving forward with your art is TODAY!"

And they all lived happily ever after.

The end.

Call to action

The best thing you can do to avoid the "right time" trap is to accept that there will always be distractions and hectic schedules. Having many things that fight for our attention is a normal part of the modern-day human experience. Relax into that idea and do your best to prune away any activity that no longer serves you.

Stay focused on the "tiny habits" approach that we hit on in earlier sections of this book. Even when your mind tricks you into believing that this isn't the "right time," continue to devote time to your art daily, even if it's for just a few minutes.

When is the right time?

NOW!

When should you start?

NOW!

If you get sidetracked for a few days or weeks, when is the best time to jump back into it?

TODAY!

7) The integrity trap

Here's another scourge that creative people often face when they begin to step out and share their gifts. The sensitive part of their psyches kick into overdrive and they suddenly become hyper self-conscious. The questions and judgments come racing in:

- What will people think?
- God, I don't want to come off sounding like a used car salesman.
- Mixing money with art ruins everything.
- Can't my art just sell itself?
- I swear, if anybody calls me a "sellout" I'll hide and live in a cave!

That's a lot of stress to carry around with you. And it's no wonder. You have morals. You have standards to uphold. You have a stellar reputation to protect.

Or do you?

Most people who have these worries are usually in the early stages of their artistic careers. Their identities and reputations are still forming in the minds of their fans. So they can still decide how they want to steer public perception. And, with good intentions, they think they are choosing to "have integrity" by being timid and low key with the way they promote and sell their music, art, books, etc.

With that in mind, let's examine two potential reputations you can strive for as an artist:

"Wow, she's an amazing abstract painter. She's really active in the community, I see her work everywhere, and her prices keep going up. She has a show this weekend that I plan to attend. I better purchase one of her pieces now before her rates get even higher."

Or …

"Wow, he's an amazing musician. But I haven't heard from him in a while, so I'm not sure what he's been up to. The last time I saw him he was giving away most of his music. And when he did sell it, it was super cheap. He's kinda like the Walmart of local musicians."

Which of those reputations would you prefer to build? Does the painter really seem like she's tainted by her success? Is the musician more respected as a result of his low profile and lower prices? I don't think so.

Even if you rationally know that marketing your work is good and you seriously want to make money from your talents, you can still be afflicted with the integrity trap sickness.

Every time you talk to someone about your art, or contact a venue about presenting your work, or answer the question "How much do you charge?" … you tense up. You either feel like a fraud or a fool, or you worry that you'll be perceived as being corrupted by greed.

How do you overcome this? I'll borrow the advice that Bob Newhart dished out in a famous comedy sketch (which you can find on YouTube):

JUST STOP IT!

I know that's easier said than done. But you must begin the process of realizing your value as an artist. You must start the work of replacing those fearful perceptions with more empowering beliefs.

When you keep your gifts to yourself, you are being selfish. When you are afraid to promote your art, you dilute the opportunity for people to benefit from your work. When you play small, you cheat yourself and the world.

Don't dim your light under the false banner of "integrity." Choose sharing and value instead.

Call to action

There's no easy way to confront the integrity trap. The only way around it is through it. You must face this dragon head on. Yes, doing the inner work of rooting out misguided beliefs is helpful, but the quickest way to overcome it is to take action. (Remember our earlier conversation about physical actions having a direct impact on your feelings?)

Therefore, your task is to move forward with marketing and selling your work, despite any fear or discomfort you may feel. Yes, you will probably feel awkward at first. You will have to contend with a choir of voices in your head singing sad songs of dread and timidity.

But plow on anyway. Make the next phone call anyway. Have another sales conversation anyway. Before long, you'll find the activity less taxing. You'll go easier on yourself. The negative voices will simmer down. Heck, you might even start to feel comfortable with marketing and sales.

And, you'll start to see positive results. More people will hear about you and your work. More progress will be made. Sales will pick up. Momentum will take place.

When you repeatedly blast through your fears in this manner, you end up making more of a difference and earning more money from your art. And that's the kind of true integrity you want to be trapped in.

8) The tunnel vision trap

Creative people possess an interesting mix of qualities, some of which are contradictory. In some areas of their lives (such as when plying their craft) they display expansive thinking and are eager to boldly redefine their genre or medium. But in other areas, they exhibit stale routines and limited thinking.

One area where I see this yin-yang dilemma in heaping quantities is with an artist's "career path." When creative people get inspired and want to take their activities to a higher level, they often get a case of amnesia. They forget about the amazing abilities they have to think outside the box and create truly original works.

This causes them to build their careers using what they think are safe, traditional methods. They choose the comfort of a well-worn path and promote themselves the same way thousands of other artists have done it before. This almost guarantees that they'll become part of the generic mass of people clogging up the old-school routes to success.

And, quite often, these tradition avenues are outdated and ineffective. They lead to dead ends and frustration. But artists continue to pursue them because "that's the way it's always been done around here" or "that's what I've always been told I need to do."

Here's a rhetorical question for you: Is that how an Empowered Artist operates?

I'm not suggesting that you automatically discard every traditional best practice you've ever heard of. Some of the age-old advice is valid. But please don't limit yourself exclusively to the beaten paths. Instead, put your own spin on a time-tested route to success, or forge a completely new path that's right for you.

It amazes me how many aspiring authors still think they need a publisher to "legitimately" get their stories and ideas out into the world. Or how many visual artists think they have to be displayed in art galleries to be taken seriously. Or how many musicians think that traditional music venues are the only way to reach a live audience.

Come on, people! Where is your imagination and inventiveness? Where is your originality? *Where is your creativity?*

Don't get stuck in the tunnel vision rut when you move to expand your career, promote your work, reach new fans, and make money from your gifts. Bring that artist within to everything you do. Apply your creative skills to all areas of your life.

Call to action

Some well-worn patterns and knee-jerk reactions are healthy. There's generally no need to be innovative when it comes to brushing your teeth, tying your shoes, or walking your dog. Doing some things on autopilot frees your mind to concentrate on other things.

But when you apply those unconscious patterns to other areas of your life, they can be harmful – or at least unproductive. Such is the case with marketing, sales, and artistic career growth.

The next time you come up with an idea for a promotion, an event, a sale, or some other similar activity, stop and ask yourself: Am I choosing this path because I think it's the expected way to do it, or because it's truly the best option for me?

Do you really need an agent or publisher to get your book out? Or could you do it on your own? Or might you publish it in an alternate form, such as an audio program or online course?

Do you have to find an art gallery to show your paintings? Is there a good reason to host an opening night reception? Or are there other fun ways to create awareness and attract people to your work?

Do you have to screen your independent film in a typical movie theater? Does your play have to be performed on a traditional stage? Is there a more interesting way you can showcase your new fashion line, photography exhibit, or string quartet?

Here's the honest truth:

There is no solid route to success in any field. No amount of research and preparation will reveal the perfect path for you. The only way to make progress with your art is by doing. Every action you take produces a result, whether that result is small or large or nonexistent. Inspired by the results you get, you take more action.

Success in any field comes down to finding your own way, based on your particular strengths and preferences. The only sure way to know what works is to try something and see what happens. Anyone who tells you they know "the right way" for you is delusional. Anyone who thinks they can discover "the way," if they only conduct enough research, is also delusional.

Artists who succeed, at all levels, make progress by resisting the tunnel vision trap. They experiment, make mistakes, make adjustments, and figure it out as they go. You should grow your career in the same manner.

9) The overwhelm trap

If you're like most artists alive today, you feel overwhelmed. There's so much to do. So many choices. So many distractions. Where do you start? How do you fit it all into your day? How do you juggle all this stuff and still maintain something that resembles a sane life?

I get it. It often feels like it's too much to handle, so you use this bewildering state as a justification for stagnation. Too many choices, combined with confusion, leads to paralysis.

I've been teaching, researching, living and breathing this artist lifestyle for decades. Overwhelm is the number one frustration I hear from creative people everywhere (including the guy I see in the mirror every morning).

Here's one of the big reasons this epidemic exists ...

Most artists think they have to know it all and do it all in record time. They feel compelled to take a crash course on building a career in the arts and learn everything there is to know. Then they try to implement everything at one time, or at least they feel like they should be doing it all to be taken "seriously."

Truth be told, they treat their personal growth like it's a beer bong! (Google it if you're not sure what that is.) They approach building a career in the arts like it's a hotdog-eating contest.

"If I just woof it all down in record time, I'll impress my friends and get the results I want sooner."

I understand the motivation. These well-intended people (you perhaps?) want to get positive results sooner rather than later. They are inspired and eager to get going.

But by trying to cram everything in at once, they get bloated and sick to their stomachs, which leads to feeling frustrated and disenchanted with growing their art careers. They retreat and convince themselves that they'll get back to it later, when they have more time to devote to knowing and doing it all. And, of course, that ideal time never arrives.

The overwhelm trap is another powerful creativity career killer. Don't allow it to gain control over you. The good news is that there are simple steps you can take to tame this beast and live a more Empowered Artist life.

Call to action

Yes, there is a better way to deal with overwhelm. Instead of treating your career growth like a beer bong or eating contest, approach it like a food buffet.

At a buffet there are a wide variety of food choices spread out before you. You can have whatever you want. Sure, you could eat everything laid out in front of you, but you never do that. You know that stuffing yourself to the brim leads to discomfort. It robs you of the opportunity to actually enjoy the experience.

At a food buffet, you pick and choose what's appealing to you. You have a little of this, try a little of that, and if there's room, you treat yourself to dessert. You pace yourself, knowing you won't get to everything during any one particular meal. You also rest in the knowledge that you will be able to return soon and choose a different selection of foods.

Isn't that a much better way to deal with a dizzying array of choices?

You'll never know it all. You'll never do it all. You won't even come close. Nobody does. So please stop yearning for this mythical state of completeness. Just do the best you can. As long as you do something every day – no matter how small, no matter how inconsequential you think it is – you will make progress.

The ultimate impact you make with your art will not be measured by a monumental task you completed in any single day. It will be determined by the accumulation of many tiny steps you took over weeks, months, and years.

If it helps, here's one of my favorite quotes, from Theodore Roosevelt. It's a philosophy I live by that has served me well:

"Do what you can, with what you have, right where you are."

10) The "why should I add to the noise?" trap

This final creativity career killer is a doozy. It loudly makes its presence known when an artist's weak sense of self-worth meets the realization that the marketplace is crowded with people doing similar creative activities.

Aspiring authors see there are already tens of thousands of self-published novels available for sale. Musicians get lost in a chaotic world where everyone is writing and recording music and trying to get someone – *anyone* – to listen. Visual artists, designers, and actors feel like they're at the back of a long line of people already displaying their "open for business" signs.

It often seems like everyone is shouting "Hire me!" or "Buy now!" or "Attend my free webinar!"

I admit, facing this avalanche of competition can make you feel small and insignificant. This causes the internal critic choir to warm up and start singing its greatest hits:

- "Why should I add to the noise?"
- "What do I have to offer that would even matter?"
- "Why should I put in all that work just to be lost in a sea of obscurity?"

Great questions!

Umm ...

Come to think of it, you're right. It's not worth it. It's too much of a struggle to get noticed and have any chance of breaking through. Whatever cool idea you think you have, someone has already beat you to it. What's the use?

In fact, I don't know what I was thinking when I got the idea to write this book. I mean, people already know about *The Artist's Way* by Julia Cameron and *The War of Art* by Steven Pressfield. Plus, there are countless other books already out on this general topic. Why am I wasting my time?

More important, I apologize for wasting your time and not coming to this realization 23,000 words ago. Please, for the love of God, give up! Come to your senses now and get a real job, before you end up penniless and destitute.

Whew! I feel better now ...

Are you still with me?

Of course, the last three or four paragraphs are bogus. They were meant to wake you up to the ridiculousness of the "it's not worth it" point of view.

Think of the ten most popular genre fiction authors of the past 10 to 20 years – such as Tom Clancy, Danielle Steele, George R.R. Martin, etc. When they were starting their careers, there were already hundreds of authors who had written thousands of similar books before them. Would it have been wise for these more recent authors to simply give up?

The same idea applies to the crowded fields of music, art, film, fashion, and more. Does it really matter that a lot of people have done or are doing something similar? Does it really serve you to bemoan the fact that you live at a pivotal time in history when everyone has access to the tools of self-expression and self-promotion?

I love that I was born in this era. I'm thrilled that the old gatekeeper system has lost its stronghold. I like the fact that everything can be made available to the public, and that consumers decide what is worthy of their attention and dollars. I embrace the chaos instead of resisting it.

Would your life be better if you did the same?

Call to action

Alright, let's get to the heart of this issue. If you harbor any "Why should I add to the noise?" sentiments, you simply don't recognize your brilliance and individuality. Whether your talents are finely honed or are still developing, you have a way of expressing yourself that is one of a kind.

No one on the planet has experienced life the way you have. No one else sees the world through your eyeballs and has your perspective. Even if a million people have done something similar, not one of them crafted and delivered it the way that you do.

Consider all of the popular self-help books, authors, and speakers that have come and gone over the past century. Most of them advocate the same basic set of principles. And those ideas were expressed by wise teachers for centuries before them.

So why do people keep putting out new self-help titles? And why do so many people keep buying them? The answer: Because there are always new crops of people searching for advice on how to live a better life. On top of that, different people resonate with different sources. (Remember the tuning fork story?)

Some people like to get their advice from robe-clad gurus. Some folks prefer the viewpoint of women or doctors, while others resonate better with successful entrepreneurs or urban hipsters. Even the most successful self-help books and authors don't reach everyone. They simply connect with the people who relate to the style and personality of the author.

Also remember this: While it is true that there are a lot of people promoting their creative output, there are also more people in the marketplace as active consumers.

That means your primary goal is to find the special people who resonate with your voice and unique form of expression. It may not seem like it, but they are out there. And you won't discover each other until you are brave enough to get your work out into the wider marketplace.

Therefore, make a commitment to adding your voice to the mix, no matter how noisy you think it is. There are people out there waiting right now for what you have to offer. Don't let them down.

Supercharged Empowerment: Seven Secrets to Living a Fulfilling Life in the Arts

1) Tap into the bigger picture

We've already covered a lot of ground in this book. If you were to completely ingrain the principles and habits that have been discussed so far, you'd be way ahead of most creative people – and, for that matter, most human beings.

But you're an Empowered Artist, and that means you're willing to dig a little deeper to build your muscles and live a more meaningful life. So let's explore several additional elements that separate thriving artists from the majority who struggle.

In some of my live workshops I talk about the three layers of accomplishment. On the bottom layer you'll find your daily activities. These are the things you do to make progress. They are the choices you make and the actions you take every day. This is the stuff that to-do lists are made of.

The middle layer above that is made up of the goals you set. These are the targets you have chosen to hit. Hopefully, these goals are specific and measurable. That way, you know when you have hit them, fallen short, or surpassed them.

Ideally, your daily actions on the lower layer should be directed and influenced by the goals you have set in the middle layer. Linking these two layers creates focus and synergy.

The challenge for a lot of people is that they either don't choose clear goals or they don't connect their daily actions to the goals they've set.

This creates a perpetual cycle of busyness that doesn't help them make progress. They spin their wheels and then wonder why they haven't moved much. No amount of "working harder" will help someone who doesn't have specific targets they are shooting for.

Therefore, if you have set clear goals for your growth as an artist, and if the daily actions you take are directed toward the fulfillment of those goals, congratulations! That puts you in the top five percent of self-actualized human beings. You are doing well.

However, there's an additional layer that often gets overlooked. This third element sits at the top, and it's the most important aspect of the entire structure. What is it?

Think of it as your greater mission or your "big why." It's the overarching reason you make and share art. You could also call it your life's purpose, or it could just be your overall mission with your music, art, writing, or other form of creative expression.

There's no right or wrong answer for how you express this layer. It has to come from your true desires. But I do think there's an angle you can take that is more powerful than other options.

When I ask some people why they want to make a living as a painter, or publish several books, or tour the world as a musician, I get answers such as:

- "It's what I was born to do."
- "It would give me the ultimate feeling of personal satisfaction."
- "I want to have the freedom to live and create how I want."

Those are reasonable, big picture mission statements. But if you look closely, you might notice that the examples above are pretty self-centered. They focus on the desires of the artist. There's nothing wrong with that. Personal satisfaction is an important, healthy goal.

But consider this: When it comes to your overall mission, what would happen if your primary focus was on how your creativity impacts others? How would your life and your pursuit of art change if your purpose was to give instead of get?

I'm not talking about acting like a nonprofit and giving away all of your music, books, art, and creative output. I'm suggesting you focus on delivering value and delighting your fans. I'm encouraging you to fully understand the good feelings that your talent inspires in people, and that your primary goal from now on is to spread that good feeling to more and more people.

That's a mission that would inspire you. It takes the focus off of you, your needs, and your accomplishments ... and puts the driving force of your life on serving others (which just happens to fulfill your needs in a big way too).

Returning to my three layers of accomplishment model, I believe the most powerful way to structure your life is to start with that top layer. Decide what your overall mission is. Determine how your creative skills benefit your fans and vow to impact as many people as possible with your gifts.

With your top-layer purpose in place, you then set specific and measurable goals that will allow you to bring that mission to life. Then you use the clear goals you have set in the middle layer to determine the tasks and action steps you engage in on a daily basis.

Yes, these three layers are intimately intertwined. But this formula works best from the top down, not the bottom up. The mission influences the goals, which then directs the actions you take. Without this structure in place, your activities and goals become chaotic and misdirected.

Here's another important thing to keep in mind ...

The goals you set and the actions you take can and will evolve over time. Those two bottom layers are flexible. But your top layer mission remains the same. Your overall purpose is your rock. It's your North Star. If you invest time and energy into one set of goals and actions, and the results you want don't materialize, you can set new goals and tactics. You can come at it from another angle. But the mission remains the same.

In a world of confusion and unpredictability, I find this to be extremely comforting.

Call to action

The best step you can take right now is to articulate your grand mission. Since that is the driving force behind your goals and actions, knowing what your mission is and how to describe it is key. So get out a notebook and start writing down possible statements you can use.

You may start out with generic declarations such as "I inspire people around the globe with my art." That's fine, but I encourage you to craft a more concrete, specific statement, if possible.

Some examples:

- "I give fantasy book lovers an adventure that expands their thinking and delights their minds."
- "I create music that inspires people to dance their worries away. I provide an audio playground of fun for thousands of fans worldwide."
- "I paint landscapes that project the power of nature and make people feel expansive and fearless."

Here is the way I've been stating my personal mission in recent years:

"I help musicians, authors, and creative entrepreneurs use their talents and know-how to make a living and make a difference in the world."

Take time to craft the proper wording that truly captures your overall mission. It will be the fuel that powers everything you do, so make sure it accurately depicts how you feel and how you plan to live your life.

2) Accept this reality

Brace yourself. What I'm about to tell you might seem like a downer at first. But it really isn't. The message we're going to explore is a key component to stepping into your competence as an Empowered Artist.

I'm sure you've noticed that this book is filled with positive messages to remind you of the creative potential you have within you. That's by design, because I think most artists play small and sell themselves short. But I hope you also recognize that all of my encouragement is balanced with a healthy dose of practical, feet-on-the ground reality.

So here's the sobering news ...

The world doesn't owe you a living. Sorry, but it doesn't. No matter how much time and effort you put into honing your craft and promoting your wares, there are no guarantees you'll get the results you want.

Some artists will follow the advice in this book and get spectacular returns. Some will experience mediocre or hit-and-miss outcomes. Many will feel like they put forth a lot of effort yet still don't make much progress at all.

I'm not going to tell you that your day in the success spotlight is assured if you only work hard enough or dream big enough or believe fervently enough that it can happen. No one can accurately predict how your creative journey will unfold. I'll say it again: There are no guarantees.

And isn't that a wonderful thing?

I can hear you now: "Why is that so wonderful?" Because accepting that there are no guarantees makes you personally responsible for the mystery dance of life and art. It forces you to pay attention and make choices that can improve your odds of getting the results you want.

You don't rely only on the affirmations you recited this morning or the book you read yesterday or the journal entries you wrote last night. The same goes for the sales calls you made, the emails you sent, and the number of new people you met this week.

Just because you've checked certain items off of your to-do list doesn't mean you have arrived at your ideal creative life. You can do what you love for years on end, but that doesn't mean the money (or the public recognition) will automatically follow.

This may sound depressing to some, but I find it invigorating. Embracing this reality means I get to face the challenge of figuring it out on my own. I can enlist the support of my friends and creative peers. I can be inspired by the success stories of other artists. I can chart my own course and accept responsibility for whatever happens along the way – good, bad and otherwise.

But many artists don't look at it this way. They complain about the state of their industry. They ask "Why me?" and "What do I have to do to get a break?" They feel ignored and trampled upon. They look around every corner for more evidence to prove their sorry state of affairs, and they find plenty of it.

At the core, their sense of frustration comes from a belief that the world owes them something. They feel they deserve a particular status simply because they have a dream or because they have put in the time or because they want it bad enough. Having this "Where's my success?" mindset is not only depressing, it's exhausting.

There's a better way. When you let go of your sense of personal entitlement, you stop playing the role of victim. If you can't blame someone or something else for your woes, you must look within. You must accept that YOU created your current circumstances.

And that's a powerful realization!

If you created the situation you're in now, you also have the power to change it. You can make decisions and take actions that redirect your energies and improve the odds that you'll end up in a different, more appealing place.

Call to action

When I suggest that you lose your sense of personal entitlement, I don't mean that you should water down your ambitions or assume the worst. You can pursue your passions with confidence and authority without expecting that recognition and sales will magically show up. It's not an either/or proposition.

The truth is, there are so many variables that can affect an artist's career growth: talent, charisma, work ethic, long-term commitment, communication skills, the ability to embrace marketing and connect with fans, and more. Plus, there are as many definitions of "success" as there are creative people pursuing it.

One artist's dream come true is another artist's example of failure. And, what you think of as triumphant today might very well be considered a minor incident five years from now.

So, how in the hell do you measure where you are and decide where you want to go?

That's your work for this section: Think long and hard about how you define success. Is it truly your definition, or is it based on an outdated perception or someone else's ranking system?

Also, do you require material markers to measure your growth, such as the number of fans acquired or units sold or monthly income generated?

The ultimate action step may be this: Be flexible with the goals and prerequisites you set. If you don't attain X right away, can you be happy with Y? If Z pops up as an unexpected opportunity, would you be willing to pivot and try something new?

Finally, even though the world doesn't owe you a living and there are no guarantees, you can still improve your odds of getting what you want. Here are just a few things you can do:

- Instead of wallowing in self-pity, choose to be positively pro-active.
- Instead of giving up in disgust, switch gears and try a different angle.
- Instead of delivering sermons on how you and other artists are struggling, seek out true stories about independent artists who are succeeding on their own terms, and be inspired by them.

- Instead of doing the same things over and over and gaining little traction, take an objective view of your habits and prune away activities that no longer serve you.

Bottom line: Clearly define what success means to you, and be open-minded about where you end up and how you get there.

3) Learn from Larson and Larsson

The best way to explore the principle behind this section is to share a couple of stories.

Jonathan Larson was an aspiring playwright in New York City. In the early 1990s he had ambitions to create a rock opera that would "bring musical theater to the MTV generation." Larson composed songs and developed a stage production over the course of several years while he waited tables to make ends meet. At this point in his life, he was just another struggling artist.

Larson found a small theater company that was willing to give his musical a test run. But there were problems. The show was too long, too complicated, and featured too many songs. So he cut several scenes and songs and refined it. The show was finally ready for public consumption.

In 1996, the night before the show's Off Broadway premier, Jonathan Larson died of an aortic aneurysm. He was only 35. The cast and crew were shocked and saddened. But in his honor, the show, called *Rent*, debuted and did its initial run.

The musical was a big hit and soon moved to Broadway, before it moved again to a bigger theater on Broadway. *Rent* went on to win a Pulitzer Prize and the Tony Award for Best Musical. It grossed $280 million over a 12-year run on Broadway with 5,123 performances. It was later adapted into a major motion picture.

So, I ask you: Was Jonathan Larson a failure? Since he never lived to see the material fruits of his labor, did Larson have a right to feel successful? Was he a champion only after the play became wildly popular? Or was he already successful prior to the Off Broadway premiere?

Also consider the life of Stieg Larsson. He was a writer and journalist in Sweden best known for his left-leaning political views. He did a lot of research to uncover and expose right-wing extremism, racism, and hate groups.

At age 50, Larsson died of a heart attack after climbing seven flights of stairs when the elevator in his building was out of order. Soon after his death, three unpublished manuscripts of his were found. He had written them in his spare time and never sought to have them published until shortly before his death.

The three books comprised a trilogy known as the *Millennium* series. The first book was translated into English and became *The Girl with the Dragon Tattoo*, which became a bestseller. The other two books followed: *The Girl Who Played with Fire* and *The Girl Who Kicked the Hornet's Nest*. The series has sold more than 80 million copies worldwide. The first book was adapted into a motion picture.

So, in the final years of Stieg Larsson's life he wrote novels in seclusion while working as a journalist. If you had met him at that time, how would you have rated his value and success as a writer? What did he have to show for it on a large scale?

The principle underlying both of these stories comes down to how you answer these questions:

- How do you measure success?
- What has to happen for you to feel that you've "arrived"?
- How do you truly define failure or accomplishment?
- What has to happen for your work to have meaning and deliver value to an audience?

Call to action

This action step builds upon the one in the previous section, where I asked you to clearly define what success means to you. While you're doing all of this soul searching, think about how you will judge your progress and growth as an artist.

In other words, know your measuring stick!

Is widespread fame required for you to feel a sense of satisfaction? Is a certain monetary reward the barometer? Would simply finishing a first draft of your book, play or original songs bring you joy?

Here's an important one for me: Did I get my creative project out into the world? Whether it's a song, a painting, or a new book, did I actually publish it, display it, or perform it publicly? That's a milestone worth celebrating.

Only you can decide what your creative prerequisites are. Some people aim too low and could benefit from challenging themselves to stretch more. Others aim too high and set themselves up to always feel like they've missed the mark.

I believe there's a healthy balance you can strike that allows you to celebrate your wins and strive for more at the same time.

Take several minutes right now and determine what that measuring stick is for you.

4) Brace yourself for the honeymoon effect

Ah, the lifestyle of an Empowered Artist. Relaxed, free flowing, satisfied. These are the things that a self-actualized creative person enjoys. And it's true. Those are qualities and states of being that can come with the territory. But let's clarify a few things regarding this bliss-filled journey.

Knowing your true calling is a special, powerful gift. You feel compelled to engage in your music, writing, drawing, dancing, or other creative endeavor. It's one of the only things in life that makes you feel complete. You're fulfilled when doing it and frustrated when you want to but can't.

So you grudgingly work at jobs you don't like or live up to obligations that don't suit you, all the while dreaming of the day you can focus on your art. You imagine how wonderful it would be to work at your craft full time, or at least have large blocks of time to devote to it. Life would be a dream.

Then your magical day arrives. You either build a creative business that supports you, you win the lottery, you hook up with a sugar mama, or you inherit millions from your dearly departed Aunt Suzy. You quit your job and devote your life to your art. You feel alive and excited about this new chapter in your life, as you should.

The first few weeks are fresh and exhilarating. You wake up every morning eager to engage in your craft, filled with gratitude for the way your life has taken shape. You feel on purpose and on track to enjoy an amazing life.

A couple of months later you have a few wins and a few disappointments under your belt. You have a big event planned to showcase your new play, exhibit, band, or book. That's wonderful, but you were hoping for more support from the local media. And that venue you really wanted to use never returned your call.

One day you're running late to a planning meeting for the event, and you catch yourself complaining about all the work that goes into it. The publicist you hired is not living up to what he promised, and you still have 17 important things that need to be done before opening night.

You feel stressed. You feel agitated. Then it hits you ...

"Hey, isn't this what I was getting away from when I quit my job? I thought this creative life was supposed to be easy and fun. Where's my bliss?"

The truth is, your love affair with art can be a lot like a love affair with another person. In the early stages of the relationship, everything is fresh and tantalizing. You can't wait to see them and you are fully present when you are with them. Your life is filled with joy.

Over time, though, the honeymoon phase may slowly lose some of its luster. You still love the person, but the thrills might not be as constant. Instead of a persistent state of positive energy, you experience peaks and valleys. There's nothing wrong with this relationship evolution. It's a natural cycle that many people go through as they grow as a couple.

The relationship you have with your creative life will be similar. You might experience ebbs and flows. There may be ups and downs. By all means, bask in the glow of your joy whenever it reveals itself. At the same time, be aware that your humanity may kick in some day with an uneasy emotion. Don't be thrown off by that. Instead, learn to embrace it.

Call to action

First and foremost, I want to emphasize something: Please, do not downplay your joy and sense of purpose. Just because you are aware that there will be ups and downs, that doesn't mean you should purposely diminish the high points of your creative life.

In keeping with the romantic relationship analogy, I'm sure you know people who have been hurt after they fall in love. This negative experience causes some to hesitate and proceed with extreme caution in their next relationship. When they feel a strong emotion coming on, they suppress it in an attempt to insulate themselves from being hurt again.

This is not a healthy way to live!

The natural highs in life can be fleeting, so you should fully experience them when they come. Be open to joy in all of its many flavors. Welcome it. Immerse yourself in it. My purpose in making you aware of the honeymoon effect is not to have you cast aside your feelings of satisfaction. My real hope is that you are not caught off guard by the challenges that can arise throughout your journey.

Ideally, your sense of purpose and joy will continue unabated for years on end. But if you do find yourself harboring feelings of dissatisfaction, here's something you can do:

Reconnect with your original intention. Once the freshness of your new creative life wares off, it becomes your new normal. It can easily turn into a routine. And often, that familiarity can cause you to temporarily disconnect from your purpose.

So when doubt and confusion arise, remind yourself of the reasons you chose this path to begin with. Make a list of the people whose lives you have touched. Think about the projects you have completed and the progress you have made.

I know this topic well. Now that it's been more than a decade since I last worked for someone else, I am quite settled into my work-from-home, self-employed lifestyle. Make no mistake, I love it. But there are times when I catch myself griping about my busy schedule or a particular looming deadline.

However, I can usually soften my stress by reminding myself how lucky I am. I don't have to wake up, get dressed, and head out into rush hour traffic, like I used to years ago. I don't have to work on projects that someone else assigns to me. I have a flexible schedule that allows me to rest when I feel sick or attend important daytime events with my daughter or girlfriend. I support myself doing things I'm drawn to do.

When seen in this light, how could I possibly complain?

So, remind yourself how lucky you are. Go ahead and acknowledge frustration when you feel it. Then redirect your energy into remembering your big why, your overall mission with your art.

Don't forget: This is what you were meant to do. There are people you don't even know yet who will someday benefit from your gifts. Don't let them – or yourself – down. Do the work and stay focused, through the ups and the downs. It's all part of your magnificent Empowered Artist journey.

5) Break the perfection curse

To start this section I will share a quote from G.K. Chesterton and then ask a question.

Here's the quote:

"Anything worth doing is worth doing badly."

Here's the question:

How did you react when you read it?

Did you think, "Yeah, that makes sense"? Or were your thoughts more along the lines of, "Hmm, I'm not sure about that"? Or did your brain cry out, "Hell no! Do something badly? Over my dead body!"?

The more resistant you are to the sentiment in that simple quote, the more you are under the spell of the Perfection Curse. And, the deeper you sink into the curse's grip, the slower your progress as an artist will be.

To clarify, I'm not suggesting that you purposely put out crappy work. You should always strive for excellence. You should always seek to improve upon the work you have produced in the past. You should have high standards ... to a point!

I understand the impulse to be perfect. You're an artist. You pay close attention to the details of your work. You notice the sound that isn't quite right. You sense the wording that doesn't quite flow. You see the colors and composition that feel off balance. So you tweak and edit and prune and reshape and revise and rewrite.

That's fine, within reason. But at some point you have to say, "That's good enough for now. It's time to kick this thing out of the nest and let it fly on its own."

The problem is, that "kick it out of the nest" voice is probably not the one you hear right now. You may be tuned in to a different frequency altogether, and that station is playing, "But I'll have to live with this the rest of my life. I want to release quality work that I'll be proud of for years to come."

Nice sentiment. But here's a news flash: No matter how much time you spend refining your song, book, play, or art piece ... weeks, months or years from now you will most assuredly feel you could have done better. No amount of nipping and tucking will relieve you of that inevitable moment when you hear or see something you wish you had done different.

So accept that fact and kick your babies out of the nest, despite all of the screaming Perfection Curse voices in your head. Your art wants to be set free. Your gifts need to be shared. Your talents are itching to connect with people other than you. *So let them go!*

More questions to ponder:

- How many of your creative projects have been released into the world?
- How many continue to sit on a back burner?
- What's the ratio between these two groups of projects?

- What percentage of them has seen the light of day?
- What percentage continues to be held captive in the dark?

Call to action

As I've stated before, the best course of action is a balanced approach. Strive for the highest quality product you can create. Don't skimp or phone it in. At the same time, don't get so caught up in perfection and what people (including your future self) will think that you become paralyzed.

This quote from Brene Brown nails it:

"Perfection is a twenty-ton shield that we lug around thinking it will protect us when, in fact, it's the thing that really prevents us from taking flight."

For good measure, here's another quote from Harriet Braiker: "Striving for excellence motivates you; striving for perfection is demoralizing."

So, loosen your grip on making everything perfect. Your gifts will never make a difference in the world if they perpetually sit in a drawer or on a computer hard drive awaiting a visit from the perfection fairy.

Also, realize that spotting flaws in your previous work is a clear sign that you have grown as an artist. It shows that you have matured and refined your skills. So embrace and appreciate your ability to recognize how much you have developed your craft.

Therefore, if you look back at something you released a year or two ago and think, "Wow, that totally sucks" ... know that what you really mean is, "Wow, I've come a long way."

If you catch yourself saying "That was a piece of crap" about last year's project ... replace that thought with "I'm so much better now."

Isn't that a more empowered way to live and work as an artist?

6) Find mentors everywhere

I've heard a lot of talk about mentors over the years. They are usually discussed in reverential terms whereby a budding artist or entrepreneur is discovered and nurtured by a mysterious Yoda-like figure. The wise, old mentor takes the newbie under his wing and reveals all of his secrets to the young apprentice.

Truth be told, a lot of people have been influenced and shaped by working with seasoned veterans in their field – whether they are carpenters, accountants, artists, or kung fu masters. It's an appealing scenario: Find someone who has been there and done that, and allow them to guide you, make introductions, and help you avoid pitfalls.

This leads a lot of artists to go searching for a mentor. Some are victorious and find one or two. But many aspiring creative people don't connect with a mentor and then wonder why no one expresses an interest in helping them. As a result, they leap to many of the self-defeating conclusions we've covered before:

- I must not be good enough.
- Nobody is willing to help the next generation.
- Everybody is simply out for themselves.

You guessed it, that's not a very empowering place to operate from.

But there's no denying you could still use some guidance. You could benefit from direction, inspiration and wisdom. And, the great news is, you can get all of those things from a wide variety of sources.

Looking back at my own life and career, I have met countless people who were kind and helpful. But I can honestly say no one ever took me under their wing. There was no one pivotal person who greatly influenced me. Instead, it was an array of people and resources that shaped who I became.

If you've already benefited from mentors in your life, congratulations. Perhaps it was a teacher or a grandparent or a member of the clergy. Perhaps you've had one or two people who reminded you of your potential and made a significant impact on your life. That's wonderful. You should cherish those relationships.

But, if you feel you don't have such a figure in your life, all is not lost. In fact, having a personal mentor is only one small slice of a much larger mentorship pie. So don't obsess about that one missing piece. Open up your mind to the full breadth of mentor options.

Call to action

Are you ready to learn from creative people who have already succeeded at what you want to do? I hope so. Here are some of the ways I've found advice and inspiration over the years:

Prior to the Internet (yes, I've been around a few years) I read a lot of books – biographies, autobiographies, how-to titles, and more. My home bookshelves look like the self-help section of a bookstore, filled with volumes on marketing, sales, health, personal development, spirituality, and more.

Of course, books are just the tip of the iceberg. You also have at your disposal Internet-based blogs, podcasts, audiobooks, videos, and online courses on every subject imaginable. And many of them are free. You just have to spend a little time conducting some smart online searches.

Immerse yourself in interviews and success stories of people like you who are doing amazing things. Notice what patterns and traits emerge among the most successful people. Pay attention to what resonates with you and what doesn't. Whether you're conscious of it or not, exposure to these stories and ideas will strengthen you and motivate you to take action.

Beyond reading, watching and listening, you can also create face-to-face opportunities to be inspired. Seek out classes, meet-up groups, and conferences that attract people in your field. Do your best to meet the speakers and experts at these events, as well as mingle with other attendees. All of these interactions add up.

Beyond that, you can invite people you admire to meet for coffee or lunch. Offer to pay for the drink or meal. In some cases, it might be worth paying for a consulting session with a high-profile or hard-to-reach veteran in your field. You could also reach out to some of your artistic peers and form a mastermind group. Meet once or twice a month to share goals and challenges and to inspire each other.

I hope you now realize that there's no shortage of career guidance available to you. In fact, I say, "No mentor, no problem!" Why settle for one mentor when you have hundreds of mentor-like resources at your fingertips?

7) Choose your illusion

Let's face it. No matter how much you strengthen your Empowered Artist muscles, you will encounter frustrations. No matter how confidently you charge ahead and keep things in perspective, you will deal with setbacks. There will be times when you feel tired, overwhelmed, or disenchanted.

And that's okay. You're human. Unless you have reached a Buddha-like state of enlightenment, you will hit some rough patches. Hopefully, they will be short lived and you'll get back on track quickly, but just know that these emotional speed bumps will present themselves.

Important note: Just because you acknowledge that these negative feelings will occasionally take up residence in your mind, that doesn't mean you have to pay their rent and feed them. Some of the most cynical people end up with a permanent mental roommate – one that constantly reminds them how bad things are and how it's probably going to get worse.

To become a self-actualized Empowered Artist, you can't allow these negative trespassers to move in. Don't get tricked into going shopping for bedroom furniture and drapes for your new house pest. Thank them for the message they have to deliver and then send them on their way.

To prepare yourself for these unpleasant moments, you must fortify the thoughts and feelings that will reverse them. If you want to build the confidence to move beyond disappointments, you'll need to bulk up on positivity.

The best way to do this is to regularly immerse yourself in uplifting messages. Read books that inspire you. (In fact, you're doing that right now. See, you're already good at this!) Watch movies, online videos, TED talks, and interviews that feed your soul and strengthen your resolve. Hang out with positive people who energize you and engage in the activities I recommended in the previous section on mentors.

In case you're one of those "realists" who feels that taking these steps leads to a shallow delusion that simply puffs you up with false hope ... I agree with you, to an extent. Maybe doing this positive reinforcement work will give you a skewed view of the world. In that sense, perhaps it is delusional.

But it's no more delusional than thinking that the world is a bad place filled with struggle and grief. No matter what your point of view, you are buying into an illusion of some sort. Here's why: There is no object "reality" in the world. There are only human beings who each perceive the world through their individual lenses.

We each make choices as to what various circumstances and events mean. Two people can look at the same stimuli and come up with two different conclusions. One sees it as a curse while the other sees it as a blessing. Which person is being delusional and which is being realistic? I say both of them have equal claim to both labels.

So, if your perspective on life is an illusion of your own making, why not gravitate toward one that empowers you? Why not choose the illusion that will allow you to live a happier, more creative, and more fulfilling life?

Call to action

Your primary homework with this section is to do what I suggested a few paragraphs back: Make a habit of feeding your mind with positive, uplifting messages. In the same way you commit to regularly engaging in your craft, you must create a routine of exposing yourself to books, audio programs, videos, people, and events that raise your energy level and vibration.

Before we move on from this topic, I'll leave you with this final piece of advice ...

When negative thoughts and emotions spring up, before dismissing them, ask if there's an underlying message you need to hear. While you don't want to linger too long on attitudes that don't serve you, you also shouldn't ignore any gifts that may lie hidden in the murky waters of the fear and confusion you feel.

I experienced this once while driving through Rocky Mountain National Park in Colorado. As I reached higher altitudes, the scenery got more and more breathtaking. I also became more aware of the steep drop-offs that existed just a few feet off the side of the road I was on. My fear of heights kicked in. I found myself playing movies in my mind of worse-case scenarios. These stress-filled thoughts took me out of the moment and kept me from enjoying the beautiful surroundings.

I stopped the car, took a deep breath, and asked, "Okay, what are you trying to tell me? What's the message I need to hear?" The answer was pretty obvious: "Be careful. Don't let the amazing scenery distract you from being safe on the road. You have a long life ahead of you."

That made sense. I didn't fight that important message. I thanked it for reminding me, and then the fear quickly evaporated. I drove on, keeping an eye on the road while fully enjoying the natural beauty around me.

Perhaps you can do the same thing. Acknowledge the feeling. Ask what the hidden gift or underlying message is. Thank it. Then let it go.

Turning Pro: The Essential Skills You Must Develop to Become a Self-Actualized Creative Entrepreneur

1) See things through

As I've mentioned before, you will benefit greatly from this book even if you have no interest in being a full-time artist. You might have a day job you love or simply want to feed your soul as a sideline venture. You can most definitely make a difference with your creativity without making a living from it.

However, if building a business or reaching full-time status is your goal, you would do well to embody all of the principles we've covered so far. In this final section I give you several additional traits that are especially pertinent if you want to become a respected professional in your chosen field.

Let's start with a big one: You must get in the habit of finishing the projects you start. Pure and simple, you should follow through and complete the creative things you put into motion.

A lot of people come up with great ideas. A lot of writers, designers and performers are top-notch when it comes to generating amazing concepts and taking some initial first steps with them. But if you abandon too many of these projects before they're finished, you'll end up being a wishy-washy artist with a lot of half-baked ideas.

That won't earn you Empowered Artist accolades. You'll never win an award for the things you hoped to do. Your unfinished art won't touch people and improve their lives.

I bet you've encountered people who say, "I'm really good at coming

up with ideas, but I need to find other people to implement them."
That's an appealing notion. If you have the people skills to find and
manage a team to facilitate your ideas, all the power to you.

That business model might work well with tech startups and retail
businesses, but it doesn't apply very well to most creative endeavors.
If you're a writer, a musician, a photographer, or some similar artistic
type, there usually is no team. Of course, there are exceptions. If you
play in a band or co-write novels, you do work with other people. But I
think understand the point I'm making: It's up to you to breathe life
into your ideas.

If you start writing a new book or a new song, or if you start creating a
new painting or clothing design ... gremlins will not invade your
workspace while you sleep and finish them for you. Only *you* can find
the motivation to make them a priority. Only *you* can dedicate the
time necessary to flesh them out and refine them. Only *you* can make
certain they see the light of day.

So make a commitment now to see your creative projects through to
completion.

Call to action

When a new idea strikes, it can be exhilarating. That flash of insight
and discovery leads many artists to capture the idea immediately.
There's nothing wrong with that. I often record new song ideas or
book titles on my mobile phone, so I don't forget them. That's a smart
thing to do.

Things get challenging when artists continue working on a new idea, while they already have several previous ideas that are sitting half finished. Every new spark of creativity distracts them from the projects that are already set in motion. And nothing gets completed.

Luckily, there are a couple of things you can do to get focused.

One, resist the urge to dive into every new creative desire that comes down the pike. I know that the excitement of a fresh concept can be intoxicating, but discipline yourself to capture your new ideas with the intention of revisiting them later. You don't have to go full force with everything that interests you.

Two, some artists can juggle more than one project at a time, but I've found that it's best to choose one as your top priority – and then make that the thing you work on every day until it's completed.

In fact, during the months that I wrote this book, I created a couple of new paintings, wrote and performed songs, recorded several podcasts, taught and performed improv comedy, and wrote a few articles and blog posts.

But the book was the only thing I committed to working on every day. Everything else was done intermittently. I still experienced variety and scratched my other creative itches, but I knew all along what my number one project was. And that discipline is what lead to you reading these words right now.

So, among all of the creative things you have in various states of completion, choose your top priority project. Then work on it every day until it's completed. Then, take the next step and publish it, present it, perform it, and allow other people to experience it.

2) Be prolific

This trait is the perfect follow-up to the previous one. Once you've completed a project and kicked it out of the nest, immediately choose another high-priority project. Work on it every day, complete it, put it out there. Repeat this process over and over again.

If you want to turn pro and have a long-term career, you'll need to make this your habitual way of working. But this won't be a boring routine. It will be exhilarating, as you grow and evolve as an artist over the course of dozens (or hundreds) of creative projects.

Empowered Artists are prolific. They consistently spend time on their art, hone their craft, finish projects, and get the fruits of their labor out the door – repeatedly, over time.

In an early section of this book I covered the importance of dedicating time to your craft and developing a signature style. Those activities can be done in private or in public. While learning your craft or experimenting with a new style, you don't have to release everything to the public.

However, in the context of this section, I'm suggesting you be prolific in your public output. That's what pros do. Authors write and publish books. Musicians write, record and release songs. Artists create and display paintings. Photographers capture and exhibit images. Filmmakers shoot, edit and release movies. And they do these things repeatedly – over and over again.

In recent years I've had a renewed interest in acrylic painting. Sometimes I'll search online for various art styles and techniques. Through these searches I've discovered several artists whose work I greatly admire. I'm regularly astounded by the sheer volume of work that many of these painters have produced. And I'm not talking about famous artists like Picasso or Monet. These are successful modern artists who are not household names, but when I search for their work online, I find hundreds of images representing many years of consistent output.

The same prolific principle applies to successful independent authors, musicians, poets, actors, cartoonists, graffiti artists, and more. The more you create, the more you publicly share, the more opportunities there are for people to discover your work, the more your creative impact grows.

I realize it's easy to apply this principle to books, songs, paintings, and other similar products. When your current project is completed and published, you turn around and get to work on the next one.

However, when it comes to bigger projects, such as plays and movies, it's more of a challenge to be prolific. Once the screenplay is written, you have to film it. Once filming is completed, you have to edit and score it. Once it's ready for public consumption, you have to screen it. Then you have to choose a method of distribution and market it.

A big project like this can take years to go through all of the stages. So the overall volume of published work will differ from one creative discipline to the next. But I hope you absorb the main message here: Pros keep cranking out work. They don't spend too much time basking in the glow of accomplishment. They quickly move on to the next project. Like shampoo instructions, they rinse and repeat.

Could you do the same thing?

Call to action

I realize this principle will not resonate with everyone. Some artists strive to turn every project into a masterpiece. They feel that quality is far more important than quantity. If this is how you think, I applaud you. But I also want to encourage you to be more prolific with your output.

Open your mind and consider this question: How could you organize your life, your habits, and your mindset to get more creative work out into the world?

When I do acrylic painting, I admit I get a little manic. I usually have three or more paintings going at the same time. While I wait for the background of one canvas to dry, I apply a new layer to another, and so on. This might drive some painters bonkers, but it works for me. And it allows me to complete more art faster.

I find that I also write new songs in clusters. I capture several song ideas on a recording – maybe just some chords and a hummed melody. Then I choose two or three songs to focus on and flesh those out with lyrics and a solid structure.

I generally don't take the same multiple-projects approach with books.

I usually work on one at a time until it's finished. But I have decided to write shorter books and publish more often.

Here are some questions to ponder:

- How can you be more prolific?
- How might you shorten the time involved in your creative process?
- Can your big project idea be broken down into smaller mini projects?
- Could you batch produce your art and work on more than one item at a time?

3) Get cozy with your supporters

Earlier in the book I shared my mantra "Focus on fans." Your primary asset for building a career in the arts is the number of people who support you energetically and financially. These are the good people who fuel your growth by attending your events, purchasing your products, and raving about you to their friends. Without a healthy group of fans, your positive impact and monetary rewards will be diminished.

That's why Empowered Artists love their fans and shower them with praise and special perks. It's one of the consistent traits I've noticed with most of the creative people I've interviewed – they have a warm relationship with their fans and supporters.

Of course, this is easier to do when it's early in your career and your fan base is small. You can give everyone personal attention. But even mega stars, such as Taylor Swift and Amanda Palmer, continue this practice at advanced stages of their careers.

In fact, it's most crucial to do this at the earliest stages of your growth as an artist. That's when you are still finding your legs and trying to gain a foothold in the marketplace. By catering to your early supporters in a personal and meaningful way, you can turn casual fans and buyers into super fans who will go out of their way to help you in the future.

That's the whole point of this "get cozy with your supporters" principle. You want to build relationships with people who not only appreciate your talents; they also sincerely like you as a person. And, because they are "friends with the artist," they feel a special bond with you and are much more likely to rave about you and support your next project.

Call to action

As an Empowered Artist, you need to get comfortable with communicating with your fans. You must make a habit out of staying in touch with them, thanking them, and showering them with special treats and appreciation.

There are primarily two ways to make these meaningful connections: via one-to-one encounters and through one-to-many avenues.

In the one-to-one category your options include:

- Face-to-face conversations
- Personal email messages
- Physical post cards and letters
- Direct comments on social media sites

This personal approach will have the most impact. Just think how you'd feel if your favorite musician, artist or author sent a personal reply to your email or online comment. You'd likely get a spark of excitement that would create a lasting bond with the person.

Another way to connect involves a one-to-many approach. In this category you'll use:

- Email messages that go to everyone on your mailing list
- Live events where you address a crowd
- Live virtual events that take place online

While not as powerful as one-to-one communications, they still allow you to send personal messages to groups of your supporters all at once. In these scenarios you thank the entire collection of fans and let them know how much they mean to you.

The best tactic is to use both methods. Combine the convenience of group messages with lots of personal, one-on-one interactions over time. In addition to thanking your fans, also surprise them with perks throughout the year: free songs, images, ebooks, behind-the-scenes videos, meet-and-greet events, and more.

Getting cozy with your fans is one of the most powerful ways to grow your creative career.

4) Let fan feedback fuel you

Now that we've covered the important topic of building relationships with your fans, it's time to take things a step further. In addition to getting cozy with them and expressing your appreciation, you should also pay attention to the things your fans respond to and are eager to spend time and money on.

Consider these questions:

- What resonates with your most supportive fans?
- Of the various things you create and share, what gets the most attention?
- What do people rave about the most?
- What items sell the best these days?

The answers to these questions hold clues to what you should focus on and create next.

Of course, this practice can be a double-edged sword. Where do you draw the line between giving your fans what they want and following your own artistic evolution? Over the years I've seen creative people on both extremes. Some artists insist on doing only what they feel inspired to do, regardless of how their current fan base feels about it. Other artists focus so intently on feeding people what they want that they stagnate and get bored with the repetition.

As always, finding a balance is your best bet. If your fans are clamoring for more love ballads or romance novels or wildlife photos, then give it to them. At the same time, you can experiment with new styles, genres, and techniques on the side. You can also give fans what they want but give it a fresh twist that is both familiar and surprising at the same time.

When you turn pro as an Empowered Artist, you must constantly find the middle ground between what you want versus what the market wants (and is willing to talk about and pay for).

Call to action

Your homework with this principle is to pay attention to what your current fans are responding to. Make note of what people are saying at your live events, in personal emails to you, and via comments on social media.

You can also come right out and ask people what they'd like to see from you next. You could even formalize this process and set up an online survey and share the link with your fans and followers several times over a two-week period. Compile the results and see if you spot any trends. Consider these findings as you plan your next series of creative projects.

While it's good to ask people what they want, the real proof is in the actual behavior your fans demonstrate. They may say they want one thing, but what do people actually show up for and spend money on? That's the strongest indicator of what you should deliver next to your fans.

Above all, don't get stuck in a rut. And don't water down your style or become paralyzed trying to appeal to everyone with an opinion. You're an artist, so you should continue to experiment and evolve with your craft. And, if you can do that and stay true to yourself while catering to your fans, all the better.

5) Understand the goods you deliver

Over the years I've talked many times about the reasons that people create. In the earliest stages of an artistic pursuit, most people are motivated by self-satisfaction. They set a goal to create something (a painting, a song, a poem) and then take the necessary steps to bring it into form. The sense of accomplishment that comes from seeing the thing you imagined come to life can be extremely rewarding.

Another reason people create is to attain some type of recognition, credibility or validation. This occurs when someone compliments you for your talent or recognizes you as the singer or writer or artist that they enjoyed. This can feel incredibly satisfying too.

These two reasons alone are enough to propel people to continue working on their craft and getting their creative offerings into the public eye.

But there's another reason that people create that often comes a little further into an artist's journey. And I believe this factor is the key element to building a career as an Empowered Artist.

The first two reasons I cited above are based on self-satisfaction, and there's nothing wrong with being motivated by personal accomplishment and recognition. But the third reason comes with a twist. It involves you wanting to create art ... *for the benefit of others.*

That's right. As you grow as an artist, you become more motivated by how your creativity positively impacts people. You become more aware of how your music, writing, art or other craft makes people feel. You deeply understand how it improves their lives.

Make no mistake, this reason is immensely satisfying for you as well. But the source of this good feeling doesn't come from within. It comes from the way you serve other people.

If this sounds familiar, we did address it in a previous chapter when we discussed the three layers of accomplishment and your overall mission as an Empowered Artist. However, this topic deserves to be revisited, because it's such an important aspect of turning pro.

Call to action

The best thing you could do right now is answer this question:

How does your art truly benefit people?

In a previous call to action I asked you to describe your mission in terms such as "I create music that inspires people to dance their worries away."

In this exercise let's shine the spotlight directly on your most supportive fans. Get out a notebook or journal and finish this sentence:

"When my best fans experience my art, they feel ..."

Go beyond generic words like "good" or "happy." Specifically, how does exposure to your creative gifts touch people? Does it make them laugh, escape, dance, or cry? Does it make them feel confident, inspired, exhilarated, relaxed, nostalgic, romantic, or thrilled?

Knowing exactly how your creative output benefits people will go a long way in helping you promote and sell your art. It will also keep you inspired and motivated to continue creating for many years to come.

6) Fall in love with marketing

If I had to name one topic that I'm best known for, it would have to be marketing. It's a subject I have researched and practiced for nearly half of my life. While *The Empowered Artist* is a departure, most of my previous books, courses and workshops typically had something to do with music marketing, book promotion, and/or Internet marketing.

Here's another thing I know quite well ...

Creative people of all kinds have a weird love-hate relationship with marketing. Most artists know they need to do it, but many of them feel uncomfortable and out of whack when it comes to actually engaging in any act of self-promotion.

For some, it's a new activity that feels awkward because it's outside of their comfort zone. For others, it feels downright dirty and unethical. The most cynical artists refer to marketing as a "necessary evil."

Let me ask you: How eager will you be to immerse yourself in a necessary evil? Not very. And that's one of the big reasons so many artists struggle with promoting themselves.

If you have an ugly impression of marketing, what you need is a major mental overhaul. If you're simply confused about marketing because you don't know much about it, relax. Over time you will easily get the hang of it. The more you engage in it, the more comfortable you will become.

The main problem creative people have with marketing is the "self" aspect of self-promotion. Over the years I've heard many artists say, "I don't like tooting my own horn." These squeamish artists don't like the idea of bragging and talking about themselves.

My response: *That's fantastic!*

Why? Because, when it's done correctly, effective marketing has nothing to do with bragging or being full of yourself. That's a misguided notion. The best promotion does not focus on you and how cool you are. Not at all.

Instead, the best marketing places the emphasis where it belongs: What's in it for your customer or fan!

When engaged in promotion, you should primarily talk about your fans and what your music, book, film, play, painting, or photo does for them. How do they benefit? How will your work make them feel?

Of course, the thing that improves their lives was created by you, so you will have to talk a little bit about what inspired you to create it and who you are as an artist. But the primary focus should always be the person who is on the receiving end of your talents.

Doesn't that cast marketing in a refreshing light?

In an earlier chapter I discussed the importance of being confident yet humble at the same time. That principle especially applies to marketing. You can confidently communicate the value that your art brings to the world and to the people who purchase it, and you can do so in a way that is ethical and authentic.

Marketing is necessary, but it is far from evil. You don't have to have a "sales" personality. You don't have to manipulate anyone. You can make people aware of the good stuff you create in a manner that is comfortable and creative.

Heck, you might even end up enjoying it.

Call to action

Once you understand how your art positively impacts people, you can shift into a more powerful way to promote your work. The emphasis must always be on how your unique form of creativity touches people and creates meaningful experiences for them.

Your job is to create awareness by presenting your talents in a way that indicates a benefit.

Years ago I felt nervous and uncomfortable about marketing and public speaking. At some point I realized my discomfort was caused by focusing too much on the messenger (me) instead of the message (how I could inspire people).

Make this your new quest:

It's not about you and how you look or sound. Your goal is to realize how your creative gifts spread joy and improve people's lives. Once you get this, your primary motivation will be to spread that joy to more and more people. You'll become an evangelist for the good feelings that your art inspires in others.

An artist friend once promoted an exhibit of her paintings with the following text:

"I'm really thrilled to be showing my paintings at this new venue. Please come and check out my newest work. It would really help me if I had a lot of people there. Please attend."

Her announcement was typical of the way a lot of people promote their events. However, when I had an exhibit of my own paintings, I took a difference approach:

"I'm throwing an art party and you're invited! Come hang out with cool people, enjoy some tasty food and drink, and soak up the funky vibes in this retro cafe. In addition to displaying some of my newest artwork, I plan to play a few songs, so be ready to have fun and sing along."

In the second example, I did talk about myself and my art, but the focus was on how you would feel and what you'd experience if you attended this event. That's what effective marketing is about.

And that's something you can have fun doing and maybe even fall in love with.

7) Get your ASK out there

Once creative people make a decision to turn pro, they head confidently in the direction of their new vocation. But quite often, even the most optimistic of them will get frustrated by slow progress. Some eventually become cynical because few people seem to give a damn about their music or book or art.

Can you relate?

If so, maybe you just need to get your ASK out there more often. Allow me to explain ...

A musician friend recently expressed frustration over the lack of financial support she was getting. "I'm following my passion and doing good work, but very little money and attention are coming my way," she moaned.

After chatting for a while, I discovered she really hadn't put structures and offers in place that would allow enough people to send money her way (something we covered earlier in this book). And most important, she wasn't ASKing people to benefit from the music and message she delivered.

She was putting out great music, but she was relying on people to figure out for themselves what to do with it. She was waiting for them to come to her. And, as a result, they were slow to respond.

Here's the reality ...

People are busy ... and distracted ... and overwhelmed ... and ... oh look, is that a squirrel?

As much as you'd like to think your friends and fans will step up to the plate and support you on their own, most of them will require a nudge. That means you must get in the habit of regularly ASKing people to do something to help you.

Of course, you must also learn the art of *how* to ASK. It can't be in a self-serving way (as we discussed in the previous section). You must always position your request in terms of how it benefits the other person.

But one thing I know for sure: The more you ASK for the things you desire (in a helpful, value-added manner) the more you will get!

Sure, some people will tell you no. Many will still ignore you. But a surprising number may start to say YES and actually give you what you ASK for!

But you won't get to this radiant state of receiving until you ASK more often.

Call to action

Here's your new mantra: ASK, ASK, ASK, ASK, ASK!

Do you want more people at your live events? ASK your fans to come. And do it more than once, in all sorts of ways – by email, on your website, via social media, in person, at your previous events, etc.

Do you want more media exposure? ASK more journalists, editors, and bloggers. And follow up with them when you don't hear back after the first or second request. ASK your fans for their suggestions on publicity outlets too.

Do you want to sell more of your creative output? Come up with special offers and ASK your fans to make a purchase. And not just once, but ASK two or three times during any given promotion.

This is something that all Empowered Artists learn to get comfortable with. Got it? Good.

Now get your ASK out there!

8) Create multiple streams of impact

Another smart thing that Empowered Artists do is multiply their output, income and impact. There are many ways to do this, but some ways are more effective than others.

Often, when someone thinks about cranking up their production, cash flow or exposure, they assume it will take hard work and simply doing more stuff. While that's one way to do it, there are other options to consider.

I encourage you to give serious thought to how you can leverage your existing creative output, as well as the output of everything you create in the future. How can you squeeze more out of the individual things you produce, before moving on to produce something else?

The idea is to take one idea, image, song or book and transform it into many variations.

For instance, an author can turn one manuscript into a paper book, an ebook, and an audiobook. That's three different formats and ways to reach people and make money. On top of that, the author could have the book translated into different languages and publish each of those versions as paper books, ebooks, and audiobooks.

Additionally, a nonfiction author could take the material from a book and turn it into an online course, a live workshop, a coaching program, and a weekend retreat. All of this from one book!

A visual artist could sell high-priced originals and low-cost prints of the same painting. He could also license the image to companies who would use it for greeting cards, pillow cases, or paper napkins.

A musician could take one song and sell it as a single or as part of an album. The same song could be licensed for advertising, movies or TV shows. A collection of related songs could be used to create a musical stage play.

The same thing can be done with the free promotional content you create and share online. A written blog post could be read and recorded for a podcast. That audio track could be edited together with images to create a video. In this example, one piece of content is transformed into three different formats.

You don't have to reinvent the proverbial wheel every time you want to create something new. Instead, you can take your existing products and create multiple streams of output, income and impact.

Call to action

Take a look at the things you have already created. Write down a list of them in a notebook or journal. Include both tangible items (like books, paintings, sculpture) and experiences (such as stage plays, live music concerts, comedy performances).

For each one, consider these questions:

- How could you repurpose it?
- How could you offer it in another format?

- How could you take the same material and engage a different sense? Consider sight, sound, taste, touch, and smell.
- How could you present it in a completely unexpected way?

Get in the habit of asking these same questions for everything you create in the future. Find creative ways to leverage your talents so you can reach more people and earn more money from your art.

9) Replace starving artist with thriving artist

By now you should know my philosophy on this: The notion of the "starving artist" and "struggling artist" are stigmas that have been reinforced over generations through repetition. People who pursue creative fields are often labeled this way and discouraged by their friends, family, and society in general.

Compared to other fields, artists often have the identity deck stacked against them from the get-go.

But the truth is, if you examine any field of endeavor – from sports and medicine to carpentry and gardening – you'll find people who excel, people who struggle, and people who just get by. Yet, you never hear terms like "starving carpenter" or "struggling gardener."

Nope. Those descriptions are reserved for the misguided musicians, writers, artists, and other creative types who live in a dream world. Of course, you know that is a load of bunk! (I wanted to use a stronger word but decided to keep this rant family friendly.)

As an Empowered Artist with a strong desire to turn pro, you know you have the potential to enjoy a viable career. Just because your specialty is creative in nature, that does not mean you are at a disadvantage. You have just as much potential to succeed with your talents as anyone pursuing any other field.

Of course, as I've said before, the world doesn't owe you a living. Just because you desire to support yourself with your art, that doesn't mean it will come to you automatically.

You'll need to combine your optimism and confidence with regular, habitual action. You'll need to hone your craft, be prolific in your output, focus on building relationships with fans, fall in love with authentic marketing, and much more.

You don't have to "struggle," but you will need to put in the effort. You don't have to "starve," but you will have to find creative ways to take care of your basic financial needs. You may need to keep your day job or work part-time while you build your arts-related business. You'll need to hold the vision in your mind while you pray and "move your feet" in the 3D world.

Empowered Artists know they'll need to find their own path to reach their personal definition of success. And they know they'll need to possess the grit and determination to chip away at their progress for months, years, and decades on end.

To step into your power as a creative person, you must leave the cocoon of the "struggling artist" behind and transform yourself into a new "thriving artist" butterfly. It's a mindset. It's a way of life. And it's reflected in the way you show up in the world.

So, if you have any lingering "starving artist" residue clogging up your operating system, it's time to upgrade to your new position of thriving artist.

Call to action

To make this final principle stick, you must approach it from two perspectives: the mental and the physical. Here are a few things you can do:

- Regularly repeat the affirmation "I am a thriving artist." And realize that there are many ways to thrive – financially, creatively, spiritually, and more. If engaging in your art makes your heart sing, you are thriving. If your talents are having a positive impact on people, you are thriving. If your art brings in revenue, you are thriving. But regardless of the current external cues, affirm this to yourself regularly.

- When making decisions, ask yourself, "How would a thriving artist respond?" Make sure you are acting from a position of confidence and value. Don't beg. Don't apologize for having creative aspirations. Don't downplay your worth. At the same time, don't brag and be a jerk. Remain confidently humble at all times.

- When someone asks what you charge, state your price – one that's on the high end of average for comparable products or services. Then be quiet. Seriously. Name the price, then shut up and wait for a response. If the person agrees, you're good to go. If they say that it's too high for their budget, then you can decide if you want to offer a discount – within reason.

These are just a few things you can do to claim your thriving artist status. Get in the habit of operating this way. You deserve it.

Final Thoughts for Your Empowered Artist Journey

Congratulations! You have now read *The Empowered Artist* and have absorbed a total of 45 important principles. Hopefully, you feel inspired and have a renewed sense of your value as a creative person.

That's fantastic. But what really matters now is what you do with these feelings of self-empowerment.

It's one thing to get revved up for a while and then relax back into your previous patterns. It's quite another thing to use your current motivated state to create new habits that will sustain you for weeks, months, and years to come.

With that in mind, here's my final challenge to you:

Use your newfound perspective to take action. To hone your craft. To share your gifts with a wider audience. To touch more lives and make more of a difference.

Where will you and your creative activities be six short months from now? How about one year from now? Or three years?

Here's the thing:

The time will pass no matter how you spend it. Why not spend your time feeding your soul and creating a body of work that will leave a legacy?

The world needs you and the unique talents that only you can deliver. So don't spend the rest of your days being a wannabe artist. Instead, step into your greatness and become an Empowered Artist!

To your success!

-Bob

Free Gifts for You!

As a special thank you for purchasing this book, I want to give you FREE access to my $99.00 course, "**30 Ways to Become an Empowered Artist**."

You'll get more than three hours of online video training, worksheets, and more.

I'll also send you a FREE sample of my book, *The DIY Career Manifesto: The Unconventional Guide to Turning Your Talents and Know-How Into a Profitable Business*.

Go here to claim these free gifts now:

www.DIYcareerManifesto.com

Special Recognition Section

The journey to create this book started with a fan-funding campaign in 2014. More than 120 people shared my vision and supported the effort. To them I am eternally grateful.

I want to especially thank the following people who supported the Empowered Artist project at more prominent levels. I applaud and recognize them for playing an important role in the success and impact of this book!

David Spethmann
www.DavidSpethmann.com

Rebecca De La Torre
www.RebeccaDeLaTorre.com

Paul Buyer
www.PaulBuyer.com

Steven Cravis
www.StevenCravis.com

Solveig Whittle
www.SolveigWhittle.com

Paige Powell
www.PaigePowellMusic.com

Linda Bianchi
www.LindaBianchi.com

Barbara Winter
www.JoyfullyJobless.com

KenK
www.KenK.com

Peter Mulraney
www.PeterMulraney.com

Ariel Hyatt
www.CyberPRMusic.com

Christine Rose
www.RogueCrochet.com

Tracy Floeh
www.PayLifeForward.org

Kevin Chung
www.MarketingTRW.com

Sue Lorenz

Mark Ferrasci

Dave Whearty

Jeff Kasbohm

Avrim Topel
www.facebook.com/AvrimTopel.Songwriter

Michael Meade
www.CheerfulDreams.com

Other books and resources by Bob Baker

Unleash the Artist Within: Four Weeks to Transforming Your Creative Talents Into More Recognition, More Profit and More Fun

The DIY Career Manifesto: The Unconventional Guide to Turning Your Talents and Know-How Into a Profitable Business

Branding Yourself Online: 10 Steps to Creating a Potent Personal Brand Identity on the Internet

Guerrilla Music Marketing Handbook: 201 Self-Promotion Ideas for Songwriters, Musicians and Bands on a Budget

Guerrilla Music Marketing Online: 129 Free and Low-Cost Strategies to Promote & Sell Your Music on the Internet

19 Cash Flow Strategies for Musicians and Bands

55 Ways to Promote & Sell Your Book on the Internet

Book Marketing Online: The Guerrilla Guide to Building Your Author Platform

The Guerrilla Guide to Book Marketing: Laying the Foundation for Indie Author Success

Mega Book Publicity: 5 Steps to Getting Free Media Exposure for Your Books

For Bob's music marketing tips and tools

www.TheBuzzFactor.com

www.MusicPromotionBlog.com

www.Bob-Baker.com/podcast

You'll also find Bob on

www.Twitter.com/MrBuzzFactor

www.Facebook.com/BobBakerFanPage

www.YouTube.com/MrBuzzFactor

www.Linkedin.com/in/buzzfactor

www.Google.com/profiles/MrBuzzFactor

To hear some of Bob's music

www.SoulMassageMusic.com

Finally, to see some of Bob's artwork

www.PopRockArtStudio.com

Made in the USA
Monee, IL
16 June 2020

32440457R00105